LIFESTYLE BRANDS

LIFESTYLE BRANDS

A Guide to Aspirational Marketing

Stefania Saviolo

Antonio Marazza

palgrave
macmillan

First published 2013 by
PALGRAVE MACMILLAN

Palgrave Macmillan in the UK is an imprint of Macmillan Publishers Limited,
registered in England, company number 785998, of Houndmills, Basingstoke,
Hampshire RG21 6XS.

Palgrave Macmillan in the US is a division of St Martin's Press LLC,
175 Fifth Avenue, New York, NY 10010.

Palgrave Macmillan is the global academic imprint of the above companies
and has companies and representatives throughout the world.

Palgrave® and Macmillan® are registered trademarks in the United States,
the United Kingdom, Europe and other countries.

ISBN 978–1–137–28592–8

This book is printed on paper suitable for recycling and made from fully
managed and sustained forest sources. Logging, pulping and manufacturing
processes are expected to conform to the environmental regulations of the
country of origin.

A catalogue record for this book is available from the British Library.

A catalog record for this book is available from the Library of Congress.

10   9   8   7   6   5   4   3   2   1
22 21 20 19 18 17 16 15 14 13

Transferred to Digital Printing in 2015

CONTENTS

CONTENTS

CONTENTS

LIST OF FIGURES AND TABLES

FIGURES

TABLES

FOREWORD

When we talk to the people – customers and consumers – who choose our coffee, they always say they love *illy* for its quality and organoleptic characteristics, but also, and perhaps most importantly, because of what our brand represents for them. They appreciate its personality, values and cultural content. The brand and product, in other words, are perceived as two sides of the same coin, so I think it is fair to say that we are in the 'symbolic value' territory that this book discusses so effectively and in such depth.

The intensity that is a feature of the relationship with our brand is the result of a process that began almost eighty years ago, when my grandfather established the company. It has had the same mission, passion and obsession right from the outset: to produce the best coffee there is. I don't know whether or not we succeed, but we certainly try our hardest. We are, in fact, guided by two values: a passion for excellence, in the sense that we love things that are beautiful and well-made; and ethics, which for us means creating long-term value for all stakeholders, through sustainability, transparency and a recognition of the full value of our people.

Trieste, where the company is headquartered, has always been a centre for the coffee trade and a cultural melting pot because of its location on the coast in the transnational cultural framework of central Europe. This means that the ties between coffee and culture have always been natural ones. Just as it has always been natural to emphasise this and to choose this relationship as the territory in which the brand expresses itself. Not only because coffee was the official drink of the Enlightenment but also because cafes, through the ages, have provided the setting for intellectuals to express their creativity and establish important movements. Coffee really can be thought of as 'food for the mind', acting as a source of inspiration with its bland stimulant action and rich array of aromas. That is why we have chosen contemporary art as our focus and why we continue to enrich the consumption experience with intellectual and sensory elements that make it even more unique. I like to talk about *eudaemony*, or pleasure of the senses and mind to share with others: can you think of a better way to sum up what drinking a cup of coffee truly means to each and every one of us in our daily lives?

The importance we place on aesthetics refers to another ancient Greek philosophical concept that we fully share: *kalokagathia*. Untranslatable with a single word, it means that the beautiful and the good are inextricably linked, and that if something is good it must also be beautiful and vice versa. This was the origin of the idea to make coffee that isn't just *good* but also *beautiful,* and why twenty years ago we began to ask great artists and young talents to put their creativity to work in artistic interpretations of the espresso cups in which coffee is clothed. The *illy art collections* have contributed so much to increasing appreciation for the brand and making it more relevant that we have gradually extended our quest for beauty to everything else that contributes to making coffee drinking a memorable experience: from the tools used to prepare it to accessories and even cafes, which represent the *non plus ultra* point of consumption. It can be seen, for example, in the design of the *Iperespresso* capsule machines for the home and office, or in the *Espressamente illy* chain of cafes, which offer the authentic Italian cafe experience worldwide.

Consistency and innovation are, in my opinion, essential to build symbolic value. Which is why our art project has continued to evolve and expand over the years. We have established partnerships with institutions such as the Venice Biennale contemporary art exhibition, with which we began working more than a decade ago and for which we produce a different project each year as part of the exhibition. In 2011 we were the first to present a work by Anglo-Indian artist Anish Kapoor in the Church of San Giorgio Maggiore. Another step in the process of building brand relevance is *Galleria illy*. In this case it is the company itself that has created a cultural space to host creative people and events. *Galleria illy* is a temporary touring project, which in recent years has travelled from New York to Milan, from Trieste to London and from Berlin to Istanbul. The project takes the form of a shipping container designed to offer visitors not only coffee tastings and the courses prepared by our Coffee University, but also everything the brand stands for: exhibitions of work by our partner artists, performances, meetings and book presentations.

This path, which has added a third dimension to the red square in our logo and filled it with content, is founded on an essential value for us all, as I have already mentioned: social, environmental and economic sustainability. We believe that quality and sustainability are closely linked, and that only an approach that takes account of both can create value for all the stakeholders involved, from coffee grower to coffee drinker. This is so important for us that we decided to obtain official recognition of the fact, and in March 2011, after a process lasting about three years, DNV (Det Norske Veritas) issued us with 'Responsible Supply Chain Process' certification of our sustainability across the board and throughout the supply chain, the first company in the world to achieve this goal.

What I have described so far is embodied perfectly, in my opinion, in the positioning we have created and which engages with the people who come into contact with our brand at a profound level: LIVE HAPPily. It is a positioning that expresses the idea of a happiness that is both intimate and shared, profound and light, just like the perfect cup of coffee. 'Pleasure with care'.

ANDREA ILLY

INTRODUCTION

BRANDS AND SYMBOLIC VALUE

What do brands like Apple, Diesel, MUJI, Patagonia, Abercrombie & Fitch, Club Med and Virgin all have in common? And why are they different from brands such as Mattel, Microsoft, Casio or Samsung? Why is it that millions of fans continue to identify themselves in brands like Harley-Davidson or Ferrari, or that sooner or later everyone will have a pair of adidas Originals, Levi's 501 or Ray Ban Wayfarer in their closets?

The death of Steve Jobs has generated – at a global level – a demonstration of the extraordinary attachment and spontaneous affection that millions of consumers have for Apple, the brand he inspired and created. By the way, the company has been battling with ExxonMobil for the crown of world's most valuable publicly traded company.

Researchers have already noted superior economic and financial performances in groups of brands that they define as *magnetic*: brands capable of engaging, of proposing an original point of view and of influencing a social context.[1]

This category of brands is adopted not only for its functional characteristics, but above all, for the symbolism and significance it transmits, allowing a consumer to express his or her identity, to signal status or manifest a sense of belonging to a group. In this text, we have defined this category of brands as symbol intensive.

These brands are able to maintain, often for only a limited period of time, a relationship with their clients that goes beyond what we commonly know as brand loyalty. Clients become ambassadors, fans, brand champions, who declare that if the brand were to cease to exist, it would have a negative impact on their lives. They find the brand irreplaceable. For years brands like Abercrombie & Fitch have been absent from end-of-season sales, and no one can remember even a single time that Apple held a sale (not even when a new model replaces an older one). For long periods, Patagonia, Volcom and Burton did not use traditional advertising to promote their brands among their community of followers. Ferrari never has.

How can we explain this excellence in the generation of symbolic value?

Until now, a limited number of contributors have analysed this category of brands in a systematic manner.[2] Many, from academics to business, consulting and communication professionals, have tried to explain how to create or maintain successful brands, with focus on mostly well-known brands of goods or services active in mass markets and offering prevalently functional benefits.

Within mass markets, the birth, establishment and success of a brand follows a relatively deductive course: through the analysis of social and market context, an ideal cluster of consumers as well as their *need* (real or latent) are identified, and for which a solution, or a better solution than currently available in the market, can be given. From this basis, a product/service concept can be developed as a brand proposition that is then typically proposed to the target through mass-communication tools and channels.

But there are cases in which the birth, establishment and success of a brand follow a different path: when a visionary leader, following his or her talent and intuition invents a product or service that creates a discontinuity within the competitive context. This product/service, and the brand that identifies it, gather a tribe of fans around it who share the same point of view, the same values and aspirations as the brand itself expresses through its products. The market success of the brand, initially fuelled by word of mouth, generates resources and opportunities for the brand's growth in other countries and/or other categories.

The economic result of these two different paths can be similar: Philips and Bang & Olufsen, Decathlon and adidas, Focus and Mini, Geox and Gucci are all strong brands that operate with similar marketable products in major international markets. But the reasons for their success are fundamentally different. And therefore, so are the variables that can allow for long-term success.

Within the wide-ranging category of symbol intensive brands, we have identified brands with different characteristics and vocations: the Icon Brands or Cult Brands among others, never before objects of a study that was able to analyse them together, starting from a common framework. In this book we will attempt to do so, and therefore provide the reader with an interpretative key that will help deepen an understanding of the characteristics and potential of these brands, and how they can evolve through time.

In addition, we wanted to isolate a specific typology of brand that inspires, guides and motivates beyond product benefits alone, but is also capable of contributing to the definition of lifestyle of those who adopt it. We called these Lifestyle Brands.

Of the many existing and complex approaches to brands, none until now has isolated, described and put into relationship the variables that characterise symbol intensive brands, and particularly Lifestyle Brands.

Starting on the basis of the interpretation of existing literature on one hand, and the presentation and observation of numerous real life case studies on the other, this book intends to:

- in Chapter 1, give an interpretation of the social context and consumption pattern that has given affirmation to a new category of brands that aim for symbolic excellence;
- in Chapter 2, give a review of the main theoretical contributions that discuss the origins of the value of a brand and in particular those brands that 'make you love them', generating a higher symbolic value;
- in Chapter 3, provide an innovative distinction between Lifestyle Brands and other typologies of symbol intensive brands; in this chapter we will also try to explain how brands can move with time from one category to another;
- in Chapter 4, give a clearer definition of a Lifestyle Brand, as until now the existing literature is limited. We will also propose a model to describe and put into relationship the fundamental variables in symbol intensive brands, and those that characterise a Lifestyle Brand;
- and finally in Chapter 5, the application of this model to some concrete – and remarkable – case studies to give an initial diagnostic instrument with which managers and entrepreneurs can critically analyse whether or not their brand has the potential to become a Lifestyle Brand, and what is required to make it become one.

This book intends to suggest a dynamic outlook with respect to the life cycle of this typology of brands. The success of symbol intensive brands is profoundly tied to the socio-economic context in which these brands are developed and used. And as the values, interests and lifestyles of individuals constantly change and evolve in space and time, not all brands are able to manage and effectively maintain their capacity to stay relevant, and, even more than this, indispensable. We hope this book will be able to explain the elixir of a long life for symbol intensive brands in terms of strategies and tactics needed to maintain relevance and long-term success.

This book is the result of a continuous exchange between the two authors, facilitated by the difference of their origins: in one case academia, and management consulting in the other, but also by common personal and professional interest in brands with high symbolic value. While the text is the result of combined effort, Chapters 1 and 2 and Sections 3.4, 4.1 and 5.1 to 5.5 can be traced back to Stefania Saviolo in particular, while Antonio Marazza was responsible for Sections 3.2, 3.3, 4.2, 4.3 and 5.6 as well as the Appendix. Section 3.1 resulted from a combined effort.

Our thanks go to our colleagues who taught us, supported our efforts and gave us their comments and critique, as well as to the brands, be it icon, lifestyle, service, cult or authority, that have inspired us, and to their leaders with whom we have had the privilege of conversing through the years.

1

BRANDS AND SOCIAL IDENTITIES: AN INCREASINGLY STRONG CONNECTION

The growing importance of symbol intensive brands within many consumer goods sectors stems from two interacting phenomena: the evolution of social identities, with its effects on consumer behaviour, and the brand changing role in a user-generated world.

1.1 THE SOCIAL IDENTITIES TODAY: A MOVING TARGET

Social identity is based on people's dynamic concepts of themselves as either individuals or as members of groups. Many researchers have explained how we build our social identity. This literature[1] has investigated through time the way in which the independent 'self' (self-directed, personal) and the interdependent 'self' (hetero-directed, relational and collective) are built in relation to the social context to which they belong. According to these social psychologists, the independent 'self' prevails in those people who search for true autonomy and uniqueness with respect to others, while the interdependent 'self' prevails in those who look for consent and approval from those reference groups they repute to be important. In this case others (family, colleagues, friends) will contribute to the definition of the social identity of an individual in a relevant manner.

Consumption patterns are often a mode of expression of people's social identities. In fact, consumer sociologists have in turn explained that individuals do not make purchasing choices using a rational logic of economic convenience (as the first economic theories sustained): men and women, as social beings, share values, symbols and a common language that ratify their belonging to a group, by which they are influenced.

None of us is an island, we are all members of communities, be they large or small. In this context, consumption is a social phenomenon in which goods are the instruments that promote self-recognition and the ties with those who share the same values and the same points of view. In the field of sociology, classics such as *The Distinction* by Pierre Bourdieu and *The World of Goods* by Mary Douglas and Baron Isherwood have shed light on the fact that consumers buy and use products following distinctive and demonstrative logics; products are symbols of status, signalling and possibly helping to improve an individual's social status.

To a great extent in response to the studies by Bourdieu and Douglas, a sociology of consumerism subsequently developed that recognises and gives to the act of purchase a plurality of logics, not only distinctive and not always univocal and coherent: relational logics (distinction, expression of the self), normative (signalling what is of good taste or correct) or hedonistic (personal pleasure and self-gratification). It was also observed how times, places and situations of consumption, as well as typologies of consumers and their lifestyles can help to explain consumer behaviour in their selection process. Finally, sociologists highlight the influence and the role of mediation from various 'experts' (from journalists to architects, from chefs to ecologists) who try to guide our choices in directions socially recognisable or relevant.

If therefore, culture, the system of relationships and the context in which we live are fundamental in driving consumption, it's worth observing how the social context today is much more chaotic and fluid, when compared to the past. Kotler speaks of an 'era of turbulence' where chaos, risk and uncertainty are the more normal condition of industries, markets and companies. In the past, social identity was defined to a large extent with respect to a traditional clustering by social class, religion, ethnicity, gender, political view. Today, societies are defined as 'liquid', religions are under discussion, ethnicities are mixed, even national football teams seem to be an old-fashioned concept.

In contrast to traditional societies oriented towards stability where social identity and conformity were used to be a priority, individuality and self-expression are among the fundamental principles of modernity, together with risk, and flexibility and orientation towards the short term.[2] In this sense, the debate among social psychologists has taken on new themes, such as the coexistence within the same person of the independent and interdependent self depending on occasions, or on the chaotic movement of consumers within market segments. Rifkin[3] defines a consumer as a creative interpreter who moves with ease between plots, reciting the various scripts staged by the cultural market.

**Brands must understand
the chaotic context in which
people live and
use their product.**

8

All of this is accelerated by the use of new digital media by blogs and social networks that allow people to express themselves on a plurality of different stages. In this uncertain and complex context, the need for an individual to define his/her own identity has remained unchanged. What has also remained unchanged, or has perhaps have become even stronger, is the research and use of codes and signs to express our beliefs, preferences and attitudes. We need signalling systems that will allow us to project our own personal values and objectives. All of this makes consumption in a postmodern era an activity ever and increasingly charged with significance.

As reported by Rifkin,[4] the top one-fifth of the world's population now spends as much income accessing cultural experiences as buying manufactured goods and basic services.

> **In our contemporary society
> brands spur affinity
> or discrimination, helping
> define both individual and collective identities.**

If identity represents a contemporary obsession, brands are an extraordinarily effective way to express it.[5] As the anthropologist Ted Polhemus or the scholar Bernard Cova suggest,[6] brands, being signalling systems with a great communicative and symbolic power, allow an individual who adopts them to share a belief, to communicate a point of view in respect to society and to experiment multiple personalities, hiding or overcoming his/her original one, interpreting new ones, finally making an identity something with which the individual can play.

9

In this game, from time to time, the individual could prefer brands that, depending on the context and his/her contingent needs, respond to a need of self-representation, rather than brands that, by communicating aspirations, desires, needs or a vision of the world, address the need of making a statement within social groups with whom the individual interacts. Therefore, as Fournier suggests,[7] if on one hand the relationship between brands and individuals is functional to the definition of their identity, on the other it is ever changing in function to the evolution of the social context and the individuals themselves. If the brand is increasingly becoming an extension of the self, this self is a moving target.

1.2 THE BRAND TODAY: AN OPEN PLATFORM

Although there have been examples even in ancient times, the identification of a manufacturer with a name or a symbol to recall functional attributes such as quality, reliability and so on has become a mass phenomenon of the last century. Brands like Campbell, General Electric and Coca-Cola were among the first examples of modern branding. With the explosion in consumption and manufacturing, from post-WWII and up to the 1960s, marketing has started to give more added value to brands beyond the tangible and functional characteristics of the product. Levi's Jeans established themselves as work-wear at the beginning of the last century, in the West of the United States, but became a symbol of freedom and transgression for generations after they were worn by James Dean in *Rebel Without a Cause*, or by Marlon Brando in *The Wild One* and *On the Waterfront*.

In Western countries, at the time of the Cultural Revolution of the 1960s and 1970s, the search for individual expression started to establish itself and consequently, so did the adoption of certain brands and products as symbols of belonging and as vehicles for the affirmation of the self. This tendency became stronger in the 1980s with the emergence of brands characterised by a proposition of articulated and aspirational added value, such as Absolut, Diesel, Nike and Ralph Lauren. In the world of consumer goods, where there has been a veritable saturation in terms of offers, products and messages, the brand takes on a social role, helping consumers to orient themselves and guide their choices especially within poorly differentiated product categories, such as detergents and food products.

Wolff Olins[8] states that in a world dominated by competitiveness and where rational choices have become hard to make, brands represent reassurance, status, affiliation, helping individuals to define their identity and make better choices. The book *No Logo* by Naomi Klein[9] opens the new millennium with a strong critique of the historical and social role of brands, inspired by the supporters of anti-globalisation and anti-Americanism. It argues that brands do exist only to sell fake promises at a higher price and through unfair manufacturing practices. Accepting this challenge, brands have responded in recent years by reinforcing the ethical dimension and dialogue with the customer through a reversal of information flow logic – from push to pull – and a new focus on customer relationship management systems.

At the same time emerging markets produce tens of millions of new consumers who quickly discover the universe of brands as a means of self-celebration.

After the initial shock, the global financial crisis starting in 2008 has gradually brought a demand for greater sobriety and understated simplicity – not intended as a demonisation of the brands, but as less waste and a need for greater selectivity. Polarisation of consumption took place between those brands considered as 'value for money' and brands really affecting the quality of life of the individual, for which he/she finds it legitimate to pay a higher price.

Man, as Maslow states, 'is a perpetually wanting animal', an animal that wants things, which will never cease to follow its desire for gratification and expression through brands. But the context has changed, and the knowledge of the social and cultural system in which the customer now lives within an increasingly globalised world becomes crucial for companies. New issues of universal interest are here to stay, such as sustainability and environmental ethics. Environmental Reports, Social Reports and in general Corporate Social Responsibility are no longer relegated to corporate communication, a means used by companies to prove to be socially acceptable and respectable, but have become a way of doing business successfully through the creation of a value shared by the company, employees, suppliers, local communities and other stakeholder categories.[10]

The phase of establishing a dialogue between the brand and its customer is evolving as well. The generic 'talk with your customer' is not enough if the dialogue is not aimed at a result. In a society that demands authenticity and value through innovation, the brand must have its own vision of the future and set out to achieve a positive impact on the lives of its customers. For Nestlé, research is a means to explore new foods that can improve people's lives. The IKEA vision is 'To create a better everyday life for everyone'. Lego aims to inspire and nurture those who will build tomorrow. The promise conveyed by the brand is no longer aimed at pleasing the audience but is becoming a binding link with every single customer. As Jeff Bezos, Amazon CEO and founder, says: 'Your brand is formed primarily, not by what your company says about itself, but what the company does.'

> **Just as a perfect filter between how we are and how we want to appear, brands reveal our point of view on the world.**

The integrity of a brand is not so much a concept to 'flaunt' as a generic moral value, but rather is the very tangible and measurable ability to do what it has promised in any customer interaction. Today the brand is a producer of content, as well as products and services. It has become a generous contributor towards a certain lifestyle rather than an exploiter of the lifestyle itself. By doing so it moves from the search for visibility at all costs towards the creation of culture and compelling experiences – with the brand as subject – in which people want to voluntarily participate, developing and enriching them. In their recent book *Wikibrands*, Sean Moffitt and Mike Dover said: '

> *Winning companies and brands are succeeding by learning to engage and co-create branding efforts with their most loyal and engaged customers [...]. Instead of controlling the brand, marketers are opening it up to exciting new possibilities. In short, these brands are becoming 'wiki'. The Wikibranding movement is reshaping the way in which companies build brand value. Traditional notions of stage-managing brands are shifting in favor of an open and authentically shared ownership among marketer, employees, and customers.*

In other words, brands are becoming 'open source' plat-forms: they can no longer be managed and controlled as closed systems, but must be open to a collaborative and constructive exchange with their consumers and stake-holders, giving them the opportunity to explore, contrib-ute, own, share and ultimately become part of the brand.

In the era of turbulence, as the life cycle of products and brands in all categories shortens, consumers are tied to an ever smaller number of brands that they consider very spe-cial, leaving others to fight the hard battle of visibility and of promotions. Brands, as tools for expressing needs and identity, are exposed today to a broader competition across wider product categories. A recent study[11] shows the need of people for self-expression can be satisfied not only by brands competing in the same category (e.g. Diesel versus Levi's Jeans), but also brands competing in unrelated cat-egories (Diesel versus Apple) as well as from participation to self-expressive experiences (posting on Facebook, man-aging a blog) or the endless possibilities of customisation of products and services offered in the mass market (a pair of customised sneakers).

In this context, understanding how markets evolve, what creates symbolic value and how to ensure a long and profitable life to brands become essential issues.

2

THE BRAND: WHAT IT IS, HOW IT BUILDS VALUE AND WHY WE GROW FOND OF IT

We are certainly not the first to be talking about brands, and numerous contributions and points of view have been offered about the subject over recent years – so numerous in fact that students and managers get lost in the vast territory of definitions and interpretative models.

In order to define the context and establish where our approach begins, we started with a critical analysis of more or less recent and well-known models, exploring literature in relation to two main themes:

1. The definition of brand and the approaches that explain its value-creation process (brand-equity creation).
2. Those perspectives explaining why some typologies of brands are associated to a high symbolic value for some individuals; or better why some brands are able to become 'loved' beyond reason by their followers.

2.1 THE BRAND: WHAT IT IS AND HOW IT CREATES VALUE

At first it was a sign. One of the first brand definitions was the one proposed by the American Marketing Association

(1960): a brand was a name, term, design, symbol or any other feature that identifies one seller's good or service as distinct from those of other sellers. Used in this sense, 'brand' is similar to the current meaning of the word 'trademark'.

Since then there have been many contributions from academia as well as from the perspective of communication professionals who, starting with the brand as a symbol and identification for a supply system, have gradually articulated brand content as tangible or intangible. David Aaker[1] introduces the concept of identity: the brand corresponds to the identity of a specific product, service or business.

According to the French scholar Jean-Noël Kapferer[2] the brand adds intangible value to the existing sum of tangible attributes of the product. The brand defines the product's direction and its identity in time and space. The American branding pioneer Walter Landor defined the brand as the sum of all tangible and intangible characteristics that make the offer unique. According to Landor, the brand is simply the promise of a unique benefit to consumers, substantiated by rational and emotional elements. Over time, and parallel to the growth in importance of intangibles in business management, definitions of brands have gradually revealed the symbolic value rather than the functional contents of the product that same brands wish to identify. In particular, European scholars, more than the Americans, have stressed the role of the brand as the engine of meaning.

> **Many theories explain the life cycle of a brand, they photograph its health status in a given time or isolate the mechanisms that generate consumer loyalty.**

Kapferer further investigated how, in addition to the traditional role of identifying the origin of the product, the brand acts as a guarantee in relation to the continuity of the quality offered. The Italian scholar Andrea Semprini[3] revealed the "semiotic engine" nature of a brand, which is capable of giving life to 'possible worlds'. This is a particularly useful meaning for the brand in areas with high symbolic value, where the brand takes on precisely a conversational collective, social and public added value.

Immediately after having defined a brand, the legitimate question might be: but how much is this brand worth? Is it a powerful brand name or not? Is it better than another? And how much better?

In the same way as the concept of brand, the concept of brand value or brand equity has been defined in different ways by various authors. Again according to the American Marketing Association, Brand Equity corresponds to the 'value (not in the financial sense) of a brand'. More precisely, Landor defines it as the total value of a brand for its owners as a corporate asset.

According to Philip Kotler and Kevin Keller,[4] Brand Equity represents the value added incorporated into products and services. Aaker[5] defines Brand Equity as the assets and liabilities linked to a brand or a symbol, which increase or decrease the value that a product or service provides to a company or to its consumers.

The concept of brand value can have different interpretations: from a marketing perspective it is the promise kept of an valuable experience; in an economic and financial perspective it is the expectation about future incomes, from a legal perspective it is a part of the intellectual property separable from the product.

Today within marketing, one commonly speaks of Brand Equity to indicate the value associated with the collective representation of a brand in the minds of its consumers, as observed and measured through market research. Indicators of Brand Equity have traditionally been the size of its loyal customer base, the purchase frequency, and lower costs of acquiring new customers in relation to the total marketing effort.

Other indicators are the favourable responses reflected by a combination of customer identification, associations and judgements in response to the communications efforts of the brand. In general experts agree that the more the associations are wide and of an emotional nature, the greater the loyalty and the value attributed to the brand. Summarised below are some models that, in addition to the concept of brand equity, seek to explain how brands create value, in a dynamic perspective.

2.1.1 Value and levels of knowledge: Customer-Based Brand Equity

We start with the famous model developed by Keller in 1993,[6] according to which the Customer-Based Brand Equity (CBBE) is the differential effect that brand awareness has on consumer response to the brand's marketing efforts. The value of a brand, in this case, resides in the minds of consumers and is a function of the level of Knowledge of the brand itself.

Such Knowledge is itself the result of the notoriety of the brand (Brand Awareness) and the image of the brand (Brand Image). The notoriety indicates the ease with which a brand is mentioned (Recall) and recognised (Recognition). The image of the brand (Brand Image) is instead defined as the totality of perceptions in the memory of consumers that are reflected in associations of various kinds (whether tangible or intangible) compared to the brand. The level of Brand Awareness is necessary but not sufficient to build value, while what is crucial is the role played by the Brand Image, and therefore the quality of the associations compared to the brand.

Strong, positive and unique associations result in determining a brand of great value. The strength of association depends both on the branding activities performed by the company, as well as from the experience that the individual has accumulated over time by interacting with the brand. The positive associations instead depend on how much consumers are convinced that this particular brand can satisfy their desires and needs in a relevant, distinctive and credible manner. Finally, the association is considered unique only when it isn't shared with other brands. The model is presented in Figure 2.1.

According to this model, to build a brand value means above all creating mental structures that help consumers organise their knowledge about products and services in order to facilitate their purchase decisions.

Keller suggests that the greater value is generated when a brand has a high Resonance, meaning that it is able to create, through the quality of the associations, a special agreement with the customer that generates loyalty but also a sense of attachment, of active engagement and community

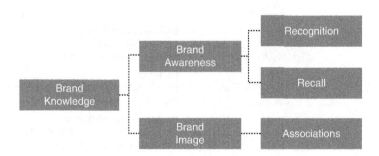

Figure 2.1 **The Customer-Based Brand Equity model**
Source: Keller (1993).

19

among customers of the same brand. These motivational aspects will be explored in the next chapter.

2.1.2 Value and type of benefits: Brand Value Pyramid

Starting with Maslow,[7] many authors and models have adopted the pyramid to display a hierarchy of needs or benefits expected from the individual interacting with brands. One of these is the Brand Value Pyramid model, which focuses on the types of benefits the customer associate to a brand on a scale that gradually builds symbolic value.

In 1996, Aaker[8] argued that from the combination of product and brand we can derive three different categories of consumer benefits: functional, emotional and self-expressive. Once their functional needs are met, the customer is directed towards other types of needs, of a more intangible and emotional nature. Scott Davis[9] has further refined this classification by placing at the top of the pyramid the needs of self-expression, which correspond to the beliefs, values and ideologies of which the brand becomes a carrier. The latter ones, according to

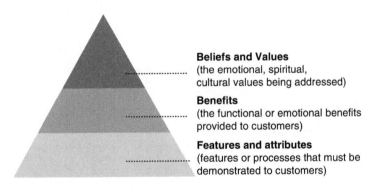

Beliefs and Values
(the emotional, spiritual, cultural values being addressed)

Benefits
(the functional or emotional benefits provided to customers)

Features and attributes
(features or processes that must be demonstrated to customers)

Figure 2.2 **The Brand Value Pyramid**
Source: Davis (2002).

Davis, are more significant and harder to imitate, but also more difficult to reflect (Figure 2.2).

According to Davis, values such as honesty, excitement, competence and sophistication have made it possible for brands like Disney, Nordstrom and Caterpillar to reach the top of the pyramid and stay there for a long time.

2.1.3   Value and brand health: Brand Asset Valuator™

The Young & Rubicam Brand Asset Valuator (BAV) tracks the evolution of brand equity over time based on information derived from periodic consumer interviews.[10]

The model is based on four pillars: Differentiation, Relevance, Esteem and Knowledge:

- Differentiation measures the uniqueness of the brand promise, that 'singularity' that makes the brand different when compared to others.
- Relevance indicates the perceived usefulness, or the brand's ability to meet the real or latent needs of its consumers.
- Esteem reveals the level of respect and consideration of the consumer towards the brand, based on the perception of whether the brand is able to keep its promise. Perceived quality and popularity are strongly related to this dimension.
- Finally, Knowledge measures to what extent the brand is part of the consumer's everyday life. It has relevance with the consumer's deep understanding and closeness to the brand (Figure 2.3).

The model indicates that, in developing a new brand, the four pillars tend to form in a sequential manner: first, the pillar of differentiation is formed, which corresponds to the

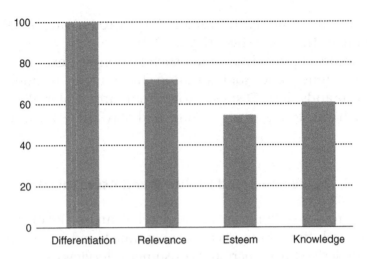

Figure 2.3 **Brand Asset™ Valuator: The four pillars**
Source: BAV by Young & Rubicam.

stage where consumers are beginning to realise that a new and different brand has entered the market.

Subsequently the Relevance pillar is formed, when consumers begin to appreciate the fact that the new brand actually responds to their needs (functional or emotional in nature).

An increasing number of consumers experiencing the brand and its quality leads to the growth of the Esteem pillar. Finally, when a brand reaches a leadership status, is well known, respected and becomes familiar to consumers, the Knowledge pillar is developed.

Together, Differentiation and Relevance define the power of a brand (Brand Strength), its ability to dictate a premium price and its potential for future development. Esteem and Knowledge, in turn, define the brand authority (Brand Stature) and its ability to generate large volumes (Figure 2.4).

Pillars, just as they can rise, can also collapse, following the same sequence. The first pillars to fall are Differentiation and Relevance: the brand can lose its innovative drive

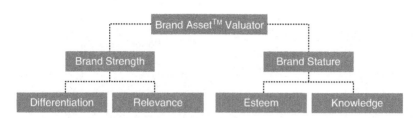

Figure 2.4 **Brand Asset™ Valuator: Brand strength and brand stature**
Source: BAV by Young & Rubicam.

or be copied, or become unable to meet the specific needs of its consumers any more. At this stage the brand is likely to be more known than preferred, slipping into the commodities territory where price and convenience become the main factors of choice for the consumer and where the brand is likely to disappear into the limbo of fatally 'fuzzy' brands. Brand health at a given time and its life cycle are represented on a 'PowerGrid', which incorporates the four pillars of the model, grouped in the dimensions of Brand Strength and Stature (Figure 2.5).

New brands begin in the lower left quadrant with low Strength and Stature. As the business develops, the brand moves into the upper left quadrant, where, if the brand has a distinctive and unique value proposition, Strength is relatively higher than Stature. This is typically the area of niche brands or those with potential. The upper right quadrant is the most desirable area to be in, where brands with great Strength and Stature sit and where they are able to expand their business through product categories and geographical markets. If the brand loses its relevance and its uniqueness corrodes, above all, its Strength, it moves in the lower right quadrant.

The Brand Asset Valuator has the advantage of combining empirical observation with a dynamic model capable of explaining the life cycle of brands as part of their relationship with the consumer. It also allows you to evenly

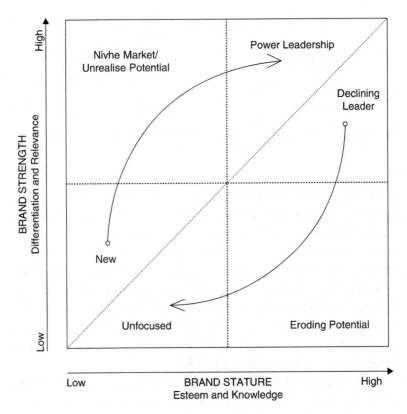

Figure 2.5 **Brand Asset™ Valuator: PowerGrid**
Source: BAV by Young & Rubicam.

compare brands belonging to different categories, united either by higher or lower consumer consideration.

2.1.4 Value and strength of the consumer relationship: BrandZ™

BrandZ, developed by Millward Brown, is a diagnostic and predictive tool that evaluates the power of a brand and its correlation with future changes in market share.[11] Once again, this is an approach based on interviews with consumers and professionals.[12] Opinions of people who are familiar with the categories in which they shop are collected, which allows the isolation of the most important motivational variables.

The main measure used is the Brand Dynamics Pyramid™, which quantifies and sorts into five levels a brand's ability to convert generic customers into loyal ones or even into potential brand 'champions'.

- At the first level (Presence) the brand is known by reputation, by the relevance of its brand promise or a past experience of use.
- At the second level (Relevance) the brand is considered sufficiently important and relevant by the consumer in relation to their personal needs and may be a candidate for purchase.
- At the intermediate level (Performance) the brand is recognised to be a good performer and enters the consumer's short list.
- At the fourth level (Advantage) consumers recognise some additional valuable rational or emotional benefits more than for other brands in the category.
- At the top level (Bonding) the consumer manifests a strong brand loyalty, which leads him to rule out most other brands upfront. Climbing the pyramid increases the so-called share of wallet, or the proportion of purchases that consumers dedicate to the brand within the reference category (Figure 2.6).

Supported by a substantial empirical basis, BrandZ provides a contribution in highlighting the strength of the relationship that evolves between customer and brand throughout the transition from Presence to Bonding. The factors that contribute to this bond are the emotional appeal (fun, excitement, prestige), the rational appeal

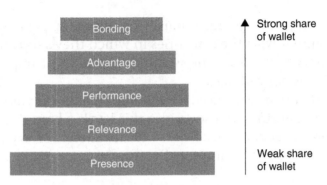

Figure 2.6 **BrandZ: Brand Dynamics Pyramid™**
Source: BrandZ by Millward Brown.

(a better product or service), the perceived differentiation, a sense of challenge, a vision of the future and breaking of conventions, the fame and money. Here we find a substantial convergence with the claims made by Keller when speaking of brands that reach a high resonance generating precisely bonding; meaning an extraordinary attachment, as we shall see in the next paragraph.

2.2 BRANDS THAT MAKE YOU LOVE THEM

One often wonders why some brand are particularly relevant to certain types of customers. Beyond fads, what motivates millions of people to venerate their iPad as an idol, a mature family man to keep a Ducati Monster in his garage, a lady to dream of a 'Breakfast at Tiffany's'? With the increase in commodisation, there are fewer and fewer brands that shine in terms of customer loyalty and financial results.

We have seen with the previous analysis that the value of a brand is greater the more it is able to generate a binding attachment to the consumer by offering emotional benefits. But only some brands are able to go beyond generic emotional benefits and create that extraordinary connection that makes the brand an icon, a cult, an object of desire or a life companion. The BrandZ model talks about bonding as an attachment that leads the customer to exclude most of the other brands in its purchasing decisions. The exploration of the motivational aspect, trying to explain what really binds a unique group of consumers to the brand and the mechanism that guides the actions, has been the subject of a number of interesting contributions that have attempted to classify the most loved brands into new categories.

2.2.1 Love and respect: 'Lovemarks'

Each brand must earn the respect of consumers in their own category. Subsequently, it must ensure their loyalty and then finally try to build a loving relationship. On this basis, Kevin Roberts, Saatchi & Saatchi CEO, has proposed the concept of Lovemarks, meaning a new category of brands characterised by an extraordinary emotional connection with consumers, which would ensure above-average profitability and loyalty.

This approach ranks brands according to high or low associations of Love and Respect. Respect is a function of performance, of how much a brand is recommended and its ability to not harm the environment or hurt the common values. Brand love, a concept originally introduced by Carroll and Ahuvia in 2006,[13] is created by a brand when it can play within the territory:

- of Mystery: by not revealing too much about itself and at the same time building a legend around great stories set in the present, past and future, capable of becoming a source of inspiration for people;

27

- of Sensuality: by stimulating the senses;
- of Intimacy: generating empathy, commitment and passion.

The brands associated with low Respect and Love are simply referred to as 'Products'. We are, typically, in the territory of commodities. Brands that are loved but not very respected are called 'Fads'. Here we are in the territory of fashions that are temporary. These brands lose their relevance when the consumer doesn't fall in love with them any more. They are simply defined as 'Brands' those brands that evoke (even long-lasting) respect, but not love. These are brands with a solid performance, often leaders in their category, but who are unable to ignite desire. Only 'Lovemarks' obtain both Love and Respect (Figure 2.7).

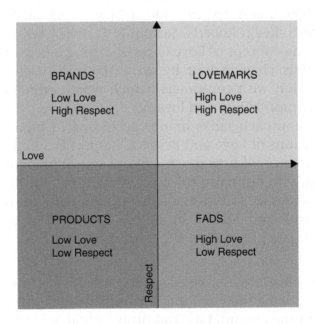

Figure 2.7 **Lovemarks brand ranking**
Source: Roberts (2005).

This approach has been criticised for the difficulty to rigorously demonstrate the link between Love/Respect categories and both economic and competitive performance of the brand. However, it is interesting because it recognises in the supremacy of Lovemarks, the importance of factors not much addressed in traditional brand management literature such as the brand mythology of and its ability to interact with the consumer from a sensorial perspective. We also see a previously addressed issue: beloved brands do not belong only to companies but to people, to those who buy and use them, as these brands become part of their world and their personal history.

A recent American quantitative study[14] has further investigated the concept of 'love' referred towards brands. According to the respondents, their most loved brand:

- is the best in all respects, from the value created by key attributes to the experience offered;
- creates a connection on a deeper level, becoming the bearer of benefits related to self-realisation;
- creates emotional benefits, such as happiness and fun;
- stimulates the desire to maintain a degree of closeness and a feeling of 'stress' related to the separation from the brand itself;
- stimulates the desire to dedicate time, energy and money to the brand.

In this study, the 'brand love predicts loyalty, word-of-mouth communication and resistance to negative information about the brand itself'.

2.2.2 Inclusion and devotion: Cult Brands

The term 'cult' refers to a person or object that is popular or fashionable in a particular social group, from which others are excluded, or that others do not understand or share.[15] Ragas and Bueno have studied cult brands.[16] According to them, 'Cult Brands' not only influence buying decisions but also become an important component of life and identity of their 'followers'. These brands are characterised by extremely high loyalty by a group of followers who show their devotion in a visible way. Based on the observation of brands like Apple, Volkswagen Beetle, Star Trek, Linux, Harley-Davidson, Vans and World Wrestling Entertainment, the authors identified some common elements of the cult brand, for example, the existence of a charismatic and courageous leader, the anti-conformism of the followers and the presence of memorable and relevant sensory experiences.

In the article 'How Cults Seduce', John Grant and Alex Wipperfürth start from an analysis of sects and social movements to identify some similarities with behaviour towards Cult Brands.[17] First, Cult Brands communicate with the market in a very selective manner, fuelling the mystery around it and rewarding their followers with a sense of privilege. Secondly, Cult Brands deliberately sacrifice a larger market for a limited number of faithful followers, who often access the brand through a sort of 'initiation' process that creates a sense of belonging. Thirdly, the life of the community of followers revolves around the brand with its own rituals, terminology and often hierarchical relationships. In the case of eBay, for example, the number of positive opinions of a vendor is a critical factor for popularity within the community of users. Finally, a strong ideology and a recognisable leadership guide Cult Brands, which give it a meaning that goes far beyond its products. The followers are not mere users, but become true ambassadors of the brand's point of view.

These approaches are interesting because they isolate the reasons underlying the privileged relationship of some groups of consumers with certain brands: the existence of a vision, a powerful ideology, an original point of view that create a sense of belonging and alignment, an impact on lifestyle with memorable sensorial experiences, rituals and their own language. This ability of inclusion of the few and exclusion of the many at the same time represents the limit of the Cult Brand, which for this reason tends to very often remain confined to a small community of followers.

2.2.3 Mythology and status: Iconic Brands

The image of Che Guevara's facial expression, the shape of the Coca-Cola bottle, the 'I love NY' logo, the white iPod earphones: icons can be defined as immediately recognisable symbols, worthy of veneration. And so are Iconic Brands, a further category of brands that creates extraordinary symbolic value. According to Douglas Holt,[18] an author who has studied the phenomenon in depth, an Iconic Brand is developed in three phases:

1. First, they arise by interpreting acute social tensions. By leveraging collective desires and anxieties, they manifest a status that transcends the benefits of the product and create a myth. Directly or indirectly, they defy common sense and urge people to reconsider rules of thought and established actions. In 1971, the famous Coca-Cola ad 'I'd Like to Teach the World to Sing' was an expression of the desire to overcome the divisions in American society generated by the Vietnam War.
2. Secondly, Iconic Brands develop a parallel world based on a narrative and a value system that, by providing an escape from everyday reality, helps manage anxiety and conflict. In the past, the 'Marlboro Man' represented the values of the Western Frontier: strong

and independent. When released, the Sony Walkman wasn't just a portable music player: it was a sanctuary of privacy in a noisy and intrusive world. The Mexican beer brand Corona owes its iconic association to the relaxation and exhilaration of Mexican beaches, a holiday destination and an escape from the stress of young Americans.

3. Finally, over time, Iconic Brands tend to embody legends, transforming themselves into a symbol beyond the product they represent. For example, although there are many prestigious brands of watches, only Rolex continues to represent a symbol of success and prestige across the board all over the world.

In 2009 Millward Brown[19] conducted a study on Iconic Brands. Born at a certain period in time or in a certain country, some of them were able to survive and overcome cultural and territorial boundaries, becoming the bearers of universal needs and values. By quenching thirsts, Coke offers happiness to the masses, Lego facilitates creativity with play for children, both Mercedes and Montblanc meet a need for status. According to Millward Brown's perspective, Iconic Brands such as Starbucks, Nike and Absolut have three qualities that characterise them compared to other major brands of success:

- they have strong cultural roots that are embedded in the values of society, often influencing their change;
- they have physical or symbolic elements that make them instantly recognisable;
- they tell intriguing and relevant stories and are able to remain consistent to their original values while reinterpreting them in light of contemporary culture.

These approaches allow to highlight some key aspects of the Iconic Brands: the importance of socio-cultural roots and consistency with respect to its values, and the ability to be immediately recognisable, which is a prerequisite for the adoption of the brand as an act of representation of the self. However, they don't argue the ambiguity between Iconic Products and Iconic Brands, a theme that will be discussed later.

In short, at the conclusion of this chapter, which reviewed the contributions on brand value creation, we can observe that:

- the value of the brand is formed in the mind of the consumer, and depends on the uniqueness and the importance of the associations of which the brand becomes the bearer;
- the starting point of any strong brand is the fulfilment of a unique or distinctive promise, which is something that occurs especially when the products tend to be rather undifferentiated within the category;
- the value of a brand tends to increase when its benefits are of experiential, emotional or social nature;
- the importance of a brand depends on the individual: not all brands are relevant to everyone, some people practically worship some brands while others ignore if not hate them. In particular, brands that are able to generate a strong symbolic value polarise attitudes and opinions more than others;
- there are common characteristics among brands that create an extraordinary symbolic value: storytelling that becomes legendary, the presence of a charismatic leader and the ability to grow a community of followers over time.

We will further develop these points in the following. Returning to our initial questions, we prefer Ducati because it is a cult: its engine has a *desmodromic* valve

33

control unique to the market, but it makes you feel like you are part of a club. You can't do without your iPad because it is an iconic product designed by a visionary leader, being unique in design and ease of use while also conveying emotional and social benefits. You want a Tiffany's solitaire because the diamonds have the highest guarantee of purity, but also because of the dream of the iconic blue box and the what it represents all over the world.

In the next chapter we will come back to many of the concepts covered so far by offering the reader an integrated perspective: an innovative mapping of all typologies of brands that generate a high symbolic value – not only Iconic and Cult Brands but also new categories such as Authority, Solution and Lifestyle Brands.

3

FROM AUTHORITY TO LIFESTYLE:
A MAPPING OF SYMBOL INTENSIVE BRANDS

3.1   A POSSIBLE CLASSIFICATION

We propose a classification of symbol intensive brands as a function of their choices in terms of competitive scope and type of benefit offered the to the customer. In particular:

1. the *scope* depends on the number of market segments served by the brand (e.g. by age, gender, price range, product categories, occasions of use). According to these dimensions, the brand typically covers a narrow scope when it focuses on a single product/segment; expands its territory when it adds profitable market segments through line extensions and related categories (e.g. a brand that goes from clothing to leather accessories or eyewear, or from menswear to womenswear), and finally covers a broad scope when it offers in different uncorrelated segments a wide range of products or services (e.g. a brand that goes from clothes to hotels);
2. The type of benefit is structured according to a reinterpretation of the taxonomy recently presented by David Aaker.[1]

It is worth describing this second dimension in some detail.

- Functional benefits evoke characteristics in terms of usefulness and functionality, such as durability or performance of the product. The brand in this case 'performs' its duty, providing a necessary function. These benefits are always objective, unlike emotional benefits, which are characterised by a certain amount of subjectivity. Weight Watchers promises to keep your weight under control. Amazon offers the largest selection of books, CDs, DVDs, consumer electronics and many products from other categories online. Geox, the Italian brand of footwear, promises the shoe that breathes just as Gore-Tex promises a waterproof membrane.
- Emotional benefits refer to the ability of a brand to stimulate emotional responses in customers during the purchase or use of a product. The emotional benefits add richness and depth to the brand and can be extremely varied, from entertainment to status, to pleasure or creativity. This broad category of benefits can be further divided into auto-directed and hetero-directed benefits.

**Symbol intensive brands
such as cult or icon brands
have never been studied
starting from a common
methodological approach.**

Emotional auto-directed benefits respond to a need for personal gratification of the individual. As suggested by Aaker, you can identify this category of benefits if you can answer the question 'when I buy or use this brand I feel ...'. A consumer may feel reassured by driving a Volvo, regenerated by drinking Gatorade or healthier by regularly having a Danone yogurt. Consumers may feel more beautiful because they use Aveda products, a brand that aims to help its customers to not only be more beautiful, but also to feel more beautiful. Shopping at H&M or Uniqlo has not only to do with convenience but also with the benefit of feeling smart in scouting the trendiest piece at the lowest price. This category of benefits is very much linked to the product the brand offers.

Hetero-directed emotional benefits, as explained in Chapter 1, meet the need of the customer to express their personality in a social context. They answer the question 'when I buy or use this brand I am ...'. This is typical in the field of fashion and luxury brands. Louis Vuitton or Cartier are status symbols, and like most luxury goods, express a 'social patent', making those who own them appear 'successful'.

- Finally, social benefits are those that allow the person to express, more than just individual aspects of their personality (status, taste, dressing style), a membership to a certain lifestyle, responding to the human need of self-actualisation, feeling part of a community, a group or a part of society sharing common attitudes, opinions and interests. The benefit in this case answers the question 'when I buy or use this brand, the types of people I relate to are ...'. Those who own a Harley-Davidson feel they are part of the 'Hell Riders'; buying a Ferrari allows you to enter the 'ferraristi' clan with pride.

A social benefit, sustainable over time, is the result of an evolution of the brand from a strong functional or auto-directed emotional benefit to an area of symbolic value creation. Porsche and Ducati were able to create a strong fan club because they first and foremost have a product with excellent functional performance. It is difficult therefore to inspire and guide social values without the anchor to an initial leadership in terms of product.

In the following section we will consider the benefits that a brand can offer along a continuum, where the brand gradually accumulates symbolic value, as shown in Figure 3.1.

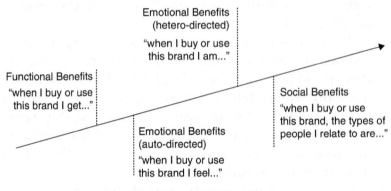

Figure 3.1 **Type of benefits**
Source: Adapted by the authors from Aaker (2009).

By crossing on a map the four types of benefits with the competitive scope expressed by the number of category/targets addressed, we come first to define two major areas of positioning: the area of functional excellence (brands offering functional benefits) and the territory of symbolic excellence (brands offering emotional and social benefits).

We will solely focus on symbol intensive brands, leaving outside the boundaries of our analysis the brands that offer mainly functional benefits. In the area of symbolic excellence we have identified different types of brands that in turn offer various kinds of symbolic value to their consumers (Figure 3.2).

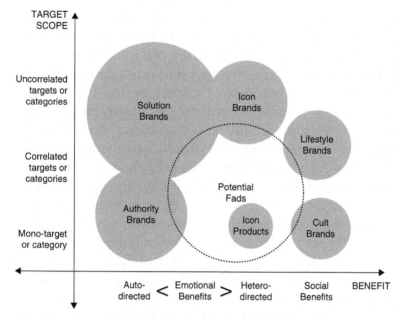

Figure 3.2 **Symbol intensive brands map**

(a) Authority Brands
(b) Solution Brands
(c) Icon Brands
(d) Cult Brands
(e) Lifestyle Brands

As we shall see further, brands that do not have a specific destination or a clear and sustainable vocation in terms of symbolic value creation for their customers are those at risk. They can be forgotten just as quickly as they were able to gain notoriety and fame. These brands are 'potential fads'.

3.1.1 Authority Brands

These brands are typically present in a narrow market segment, providing prevalently auto-directed emotional benefits, designed therefore for personal satisfaction and pleasure. These are specialised brands, considered as a real authority in their segment. They often focus on patents, innovation and distinctive styles or products (e.g. the special 'interwoven' process of leather by the luxury brand Bottega Veneta), and are enriched by experiential product benefits. Victorinox, Illy and BlackBerry belong to this category, as well as the Dr Hauschka cosmetics brand, an authority for the integrity in its process and purity of the ingredients. These are brands that have the power to influence and persuade by virtue of their particular expertise. By adopting these brands you feel reassured and gratified, a benefit that goes beyond the functional aspect.

This competence, both superior and distinctive, is often the starting point towards developing into other types of brands: Iconic, Cult or Lifestyle Brands often take origin from a niche where they have developed a successful product that has become the reference of their category, and from that position of authority have moved to other dimensions in our map. Hermès was and still is an 'authority' as luxury saddler, but it has steadily moved into an Iconic Brand position by adding new product segments to emotional benefits that gradually evolved into a more hetero-directed dimension of status. Technological integration, the continuous and obsessive search for ergonomics and the beauty of shapes, the meticulous care and craftsmanship in the construction that have remained unchanged for nearly a century of activity, have transformed Leica from an 'authority' in the area of photography to a Cult Brand – a Leica 0-Serie Nr.107 (1923) camera was sold for 1.3 million EUR at Westilicht Photographica Auctions in 2012 to a private Asian collector.

For cosmetics and personal care products, authority provides permission to hope. Authority can come from an ingredient, a brand ambassador, a legend. 'Miracle Broth' is an elixir based of sea kelp and bio-fermentation, known for its healing energies, which powers the most luxurious brand in beauty, La Mer. Clinique, owned by the Estee Lauder Group, is the first ever dermatologist-created cosmetic brand and a leading skincare authority, with all its skincare products Allergy Tested and 100% Fragrance Free.

The Authority status may be acquired through skills accumulated over generations or even in the short term through product or process innovations, but in any case must be constantly maintained through time and protected both from obsolescence and attacks by competitors.

3.1.2 Solution Brands

In a similar way to Authority Brands, Solution Brands provide primarily auto-directed emotional benefits ('when I buy or use this brand I feel ...'), but unlike them they now turn to a broader market, covering various segments of consumers through a wider selection of products.

Solution Brands are generally very respected and offer a completely satisfying solution within many product categories (think, for example, of Philips in consumer electronics), independently of whether they operate in a mass or premium market. This category includes many of the best-known brands, which typically occupy a leading position and offer a wide range of products in very competitive and cluttered sectors, such as Microsoft, Sony and Mattel, but also includes brands like Honda and Nokia. Often, they have become Solution Brands by starting from a position of 'authority' based on a highly successful innovation, like the operating system MS-DOS for Microsoft or the use of plastic in luggage for Samsonite, then have moved to an Iconic or Cult Brand stage with products that have marked an era or have been an object of desire for a generation or more, such as the Beetle, Barbie, Walkman or Levi's 501. Thanks to this legacy many Solution Brands still manage to provide their customers with emotional auto-directed benefits after many years. Others have lost symbolic value while still maintaining the ability to satisfy emotional auto-directed needs (e.g. needs for reassurance and conformity) for millions of consumers with an extensive offer and a global presence.

3.1.3 Icon Brands and Style Icons

Within the universe of symbolic brands, Icon Brands become the carriers of universal values and stories that they express through a range of products characterised by instantly recognisable and iconic codes. Adopting these brands is a statement that generates emotional hetero-directed benefits for the consumer ('when I buy or use this brand, I am ...'). Icons are timeless: even those born as phenomena of fashion, once gaining the status of icon, avoid the fashion cliché. This happened for the French luxury brands (such as Chanel and Hermès) or for globally admired jewellers such as Bulgari, Cartier and Tiffany: fashion brands become iconic when they are able to move beyond fashion by offering the iconic elements that have made them successful over time in products, communication and in-store. Since the 1950s, Bulgari has been identified by the ornamental 'parenthesis' design that, when applied in jewellery and glasses, recalls ancient Roman roads; for Cartier the 'animalier' motif that was so liked by maharajahs and princesses speaks of and recalls a luxury that no longer exists but many still aspire to. Besides fashion, Armani has become an icon of Italian style and understated elegance that is found in the wide range of products, from clothing to perfumes, linked to the first line of the designer.

As mentioned, Icon Brands often come from a position of 'authority' or 'cult', extending the range of products and their popularity outside a more or less restricted circle of followers. At the height of their success, they become well-known brands, both loved and desired, and success is mainly determined by their ability to be in tune with the deep values that people share, often going beyond age and geographical boundaries. These value generally evolve slowly but, as noted by Holt,[2] when deep cultural changes occur the mythology of Icon Brands loses relevance and people go in search of a new myth. But, at the same time, Icon Brands cannot betray the core values that brought them success to pursue business opportunities that do not belong to them. In the late 1990s clothing brand Gap was an icon of American casual style, namely 'an American classic with a twist.' After fast fashion chains entered the market, Gap decided to follow in their footsteps, quickly losing its iconic status and for some years also its economic success.

While European luxury brands can be excellent authorities (e.g. Berluti shoes), cults (Riva motorboats) or icons (Hermès), the fashion houses such as Dior, Gucci or Dolce & Gabbana are brand typologies that are harder to classify. By often founding their authority on a style expression rather than on product features they were able to offer, often from the very beginning, a wide range of products. Strictly speaking they are not Icon Brands because they follow the changes in fashion; and they are not Lifestyle Brands because they don't necessarily offer a perspective on the world and a call to action. They aren't a Solution Brand, given they offer hetero-directed benefits. We refer to these types of brands as 'Style Icons'. They require constant evolution while maintaining their characteristic expressive codes intact. Brands such as Prada or Stella McCartney are always ahead of the fashion – in fact, they must create the

43

fashion that subsequently others will follow, even if in the end the products that ultimately sell are the most recognisable in materials, details, forms, and in fact style.

> **In fashion,**
> **we can identify**
> **Style Icons.**

Style Icons are different from Icon Brands because:

- they refer to values of elegance, status and clothing styles that have higher volatility and sensitivity to changes in customs and tastes;
- they are particularly influenced by the processes of 'viral' diffusion – they have cycles of adoption, development, success and decline that are much faster than for other types of brands, especially the Icons.

When their leader (typically a fashion designer) leaves the company or passes away, these brands tend to lose the ability to anticipate or influence clothing market trends, or gradually disappear becoming less relevant, or are repositioned starting a new cycle based on iconic elements of the past, as has happened in the case of Moschino, Gucci, Dior and Versace.

3.1.4 Icon Products

A further aspect of the Icon Brands has not yet been adequately treated in the academic literature: the same ability to offer emotional benefits can be associated with only one product (Absolut Vodka) or a product line that insists on a very limited market segment, as in the event of Mini. In this case we speak of Icon Products and move vertically to the bottom of our diagram. There are brands where the Iconic Product coincides with that same brand, such as Havaianas, Moleskine, Nespresso or Red Bull. There are also Solution Brands that have within their wide range of products an Iconic one, such as the Fiat 500, or the classic Lacoste piquet shirt. Another case is that of some furniture brands, which, by working with great designers, have in their portfolios many Iconic Products while not being necessarily Icon Brands themselves. For example, the Italian lighting design company Flos produces Icons such as the Glo-Ball lamp designed by Jasper Morrison, or the KTribe lamp designed by Philip Stark. The Italian furniture manufacturer Cassina still produces the famous 'Fauteuil Gran Comfort' sofa line originally designed in 1929 by Le Corbusier. Other brands that were born instead as an authority in a special type of manufacturing (e.g. leather for Poltrona Frau) or in materials used (e.g. coloured plastic for Kartell), have subsequently established iconic products through collaboration with renowned designers, and then tried to move into the Iconic Brands territory by widening the range of products and communicating the world of the brand.

> **The furniture industry is
> characterised by Icon Products.**

An Icon Brand almost always starts off with an Iconic Product that is emblematic of its DNA and for that reason subsequently gets reproposed in the brand's communication or seasonal offers, sometimes reinterpreted in contemporary materials and styles: think of the Hermès

Kelly bag, the Wayfarer model by Ray-Ban, the Oyster by Rolex, the Chanel blazer or Tod's loafers. It is also possible, however, that an Iconic Product fails to generate an Iconic Brand, because it is not rich enough in emotional content or because the brand extension fails: this is the case for the Italian shoe brand Superga, who never managed to move away from the iconic white sneakers, a jump that was successfully managed by Nike and Adidas. In contrast, a larger and successful proposition was built around the iconic CK One fragrance, which nowadays is challenging in popularity the same mother brand, Calvin Klein.

3.1.5 Cult Brands

Among the brands oriented towards symbolic excellence, Cult Brands are specialised and are very much tied to a single category or a specific market segment. These brands have the ability to offer a social benefit ('when I buy or use this brand, the type of people I relate to are ...') to specific communities of consumers who share certain values and passions, such as cigar smokers, golfers, bikers, watch collectors, rock guitarists, sailors and so on. For these categories of people brands like Triumph, Ping, Cohiba, Breguet, Fender and Nautor's Swan generate almost a passion with pathological features, which needs to be shared.

For sailors around the world, Nautor's Swan yachts manufacturer holds a unique place in their hearts. Pekka Koskenkyla's (Nautor's Finnish founder) vision of combining traditional craftsmanship and age-old traditions with the most advanced technologies flourishes when nurtured by the sense of mysticism and the hardworking ethos that surrounds Nordic culture. Every Swan owner becomes a ClubSwan member, with the opportunity to share experiences with other owners at a broad range of Nautor's Swan events staged in the most exclusive destinations around the globe.

All these brands promote social activities and sharing of experiences among their respective customers. Unlike Authority Brands, Cult Brands do not base their strength on only single-product expertise, but also (and especially) on their ability to create affiliation and a sense of belonging through their adoption. A widely cited example is Harley-Davidson. Although the bikes themselves are not the most advanced on the market in terms of technology, comfort and drivability, Harley-Davidson customers still prefer the brand because they embrace the open roads, free spirit mythology and the macho connotations of the Hells Angels, which are well expressed in terms of product with the low seat near the engine, offering a feeling of power. They are so much more than just loyal customers because they simply cannot find other brands that can better embody the lifestyle to which they contribute and are inspired by, idolising the unmistakable roar of the engine and sometimes getting the logo tattooed on their skin.[3]

For Cult Brands, anecdotes that fuel storytelling are essential. In the 1960s the historic arrival of three Ferraris aligned at the 24 Hours of Daytona has done more than any advertising campaign for the brand's success in a strategic market such as the United States. The parade of a Ferrari gathering is always an event to talk about, wherever it happens in any corner of the world. And the fact that the motor shaft, the heart of the engine of a Ferrari, is still balanced and finished by hand is a story that fascinates legions of fans. Moving through the Cult phase is typical of many brands that become Icons or Lifestyle, but even in this case, the brand maintains an original core of fans who give authenticity to the brand and remain its most important ambassadors.

3.1.6 Lifestyle Brands

Today the word lifestyle suggests a way of life to which people associate patterns of relationships, behaviour and especially of consumption.

In our approach, Lifestyle Brands are able to generate a social benefit ('when I buy or use this brand, the type of people I relate to are …') on a relatively high number of business segments, becoming a recognised phenomenon. These are brands that are the bearers of an ideology, which dictates the rules, or that indicates a way of life, and are able to express it in an original way in different categories.

Patagonia offers an environmentally friendly way of life. With Nike one enters the community of those who want to push their limits. Volcom, with the promise 'Youth Against Establishment', gives a label and a sense of belonging to those who are 'against' the world of adults. When it appears, a Lifestyle Brand typically covers a semantic territory, creating a disruption with the status quo and proposing an innovative viewpoint on the world. The driver may be the product (e.g. The Body Shop with natural cosmetics), the shopping experience (e.g. Abercrombie & Fitch with its stores), the service (e.g. Club Med), the communication (e.g. Diesel) or a combination of these elements.

A Lifestyle Brand almost always takes energy from the world of youngsters to assert and enforce the change. Brands like Apple, Burton, Virgin and Nike initially took on a community of kids/young adults, convincing an increasingly growing number of people that their adoption would reinforce and amplify their ethos, their culture and their social identity.

For a brand, a clear indication of the Lifestyle status is the existence of a call to action, a rallying cry urging the faithful to be the bearers of a movement, a vision of the future conveyed through an active attitude. 'Just Do It!' (Nike) and, subsequently, more provocatively, 'Be Stupid!' (Diesel), 'Think Different' (Apple) and 'Walk Don't Run' (Camper) are now historical examples of something more than a simple slogan or a tagline.

Like Cult Brands, Lifestyle Brands almost always originate from the insight of a visionary leader who anticipates a deep and keen social need. In this case, this intuition does not remain closed within of a circle of followers; on the contrary, it generates a broader value. Compared to Icon Brands, Lifestyle Brands maintain a strongly dynamic perspective, always remaining in motion and fuelling their own point of view of the world. Icon Brands instead tend to crystallise in their own legend. To continue the Nike case study, the same company's CEO, Mark Parker, is said to draw inspiration from everything, every place and every person, personifying one of the golden rules of the brand: 'Be a sponge. Curiosity is life. Assumption is death. Look around.' At the conclusion of this classification of symbol intensive brands, in Table 3.1, we propose a visualisation and synthesis of what are the particular features of different types of brands. We also propose some specific modes of assessment that may better characterise the ascription of the brand to a particular category.

3.2 A DYNAMIC MODEL: HOW BRANDS MOVE WITHIN THE MAP

Our model doesn't try to (nor should) oversimplify a reality that is complex. A shift of the brand is possible, indeed highly likely, in terms of product range and associated benefits, through the different territories of the map over time and across different countries and cultures.

TABLE 3.1 **Features and characteristics of symbol intensive brands**

Brand typology	Scope	Benefit typology	Measurement	Example
Authority	Narrow	Emotional, Auto-directed	Existence of a product narrative, facts that establish technical or experiential superiority of the product, the presence of a leader with product authority	LoroPiana, Illy, Leica, BlackBerry
Cult	Narrow	Social	Existence of a brand narrative, existence of a community of fans of a specific product category, existence of rituals and gatherings, continuous dialogue both on and offline between brand and customers	Ferrari, Porsche, Harley-Davidson, Fender, Cohiba, Nautor Swan
Solution	Broad target/ categories, correlated and non-correlated	Emotional, Auto-directed	Top-of-mind brand within a wide product range. Existence of a product, service, value proposition narrative	Gap, Mattel, Sony, Microsoft
Icon Brand, (and Style Icons)	Broad target/ categories, correlated	Emotional, Hetero-directed	Existence of a brand heritage and mythology; presence of the brand or clothing styles (Style icons) in popular culture	Chanel, Tiffany, Hermès, Adidas Prada, Dolce & Gabbana (Style Icons)
Icon Product	Narrow	Emotional, Hetero-directed	Existence of a product mythology; presence of the product in popular culture	Mini, Vespa, Coca-Cola
Lifestyle	Broad target/ categories, correlated	Social	Existence of a brand narrative presented as storytelling, high contribution to current lifestyles, presence of a call to action, existence of creative and visionary leaders, importance of word of mouth	Diesel, Apple, Virgin, Slow Food, Patagonia

We cannot predict that brands will develop in a purely linear way, for example from Authority to Lifestyle, but we should take into account possible vertical and circular paths in the map. For example, Coca-Cola was introduced in a pharmacy in response to a functional need and subsequently became an Icon Product, known in every corner of the planet. In the golden years of Hi-Fi, Pioneer established itself as an Authority before becoming a Solution Brand covering a larger number of market segments, from radio to television and home theatre systems. Marlboro, which is definitely an Icon Product in its core business of cigarettes, tried to establish itself as an Icon Brand by transferring the values and emotional benefits to the leisure wear market through the Marlboro Classics line. However, as a result of campaigns and policies to combat smoking, it was forced to abandon the extension and refocus on the core business and on its Iconic Product with the Malboro name.

Brands live in a dynamic context, moving within the symbol intensive brands map.

Burberry started as an Authority Brand in outerwear as a supplier to the British Royal Air Force and the royal family. It developed an Iconic Product, the trench coat, holding a strong visual code, the tartan check, which was applied to all clothing and accessories. This brought the brand to become initially a trend and then a fad in the 1990s. Since 1997, the repositioning has gone in the direction of proposing a more youthful and dynamic British contemporary lifestyle, well interpreted by the testimonial Kate Moss, one of the few models that also embody a lifestyle. As with many other menswear clothing brands, Ermenegildo Zegna was established as an Authority Brand initially in woollen fabrics, then subsequently with formalwear. Thanks to the vision of the third generation of the Zegna family, the brand has gradually moved into Style Icons' territory by widening the range of products from clothing to accessories and perfumes and introducing new lines such as Zegna Soft and Zegna Sport for different targets and occasions of use. The brand wanted to establish itself as an icon of Italian style in luxury, leveraging hetero-directed benefits in terms of elegance and status while celebrating its hundred-year heritage.

It is also common for a brand to occupy different positions in the map depending on the perception of consumers in different countries, given how the symbolic value of an element varies across cultures. For a long time, Levi's was seen as an Icon Product in Europe and a Solution Brand in the American market. McDonald's may be regarded as an Icon Brand in some emerging countries and a Solution Brand in other more mature markets.

Similarly, it may happen that a brand has a different placement in the map depending on the category: in the early 2000s, Fila sneakers were a Cult Brand for African-Americans in major US metropolitan areas, a Solution Brand in Europe for apparel, and an Icon Brand for the same apparel market in Asia. This was most definitely a difficult situation to manage.

3.3 KNOWING WHERE TO GO TO NOT DISAPPEAR: THE FADING RISK

It is crucial that each brand tends towards a unique direction, a precise calling to one of the five types of brands and symbolic territories that we have indicated on the map, and not remain, in other words, 'stuck in the middle'. For example, a well-known brand such as Calvin Klein, born as a New York Cult Brand with a successful line of jeans and perfumes, became a Style Icon that interpreted emerging themes of sexuality and transgression in the 1990s. However, when these themes lost social relevance the brand itself lost direction and iconic status, becoming an empire of licences, many of which were meaningless and lacked economic success.

The American brand Crocs launched clogs in a plastic resin (Croslite), both light and colourful, which suddenly become a global phenomenon. Within a few years, competitors saturated the market with lower-priced imitations. To avoid the risk of being just a fad, the brand was extended in terms of occasions of use (winter usage), was invested in other product categories (clothing) by trying to transfer innovation in terms of material, explored new segments where clogs could be functional (such as clothing for hospitals) and launched a customisable line.

Is such a strategy a suitable solution? Not always: the challenge lies in seeing whether, besides product extensions, the brand will be able to create unique and sustainable emotional benefits for its clients, or even inspire a lifestyle. The example could be extended to many brands in the fashion industry that seek to occupy many categories, even through secondary and licensed brands, and diluting their integrity over time as well as their iconic status.

**Many successful brands
fail to anchor themselves
to a sustainable way of generating symbolic
value for the customer, remaining
at the stage of a short-term phenomenon.**

The same is also true for those brands that remain slaves to the fashion effect and to consumer satisfaction in terms of single seasonal collections, which they promote heavily with a continuous and systematic presence in the media but still struggle to build a brand equity that goes beyond a general recall (brand awareness).

In the map we define these types of symbolic brands as 'Potential Fads': brands or products that offer hetero-directed benefits. Sometimes they take the dimension of a pure phenomenon, but then fail to find a sustainable way to maintain value creation for consumers and long term-success. On the contrary, this being the thesis of this book, the five different brand typologies we have identified in our map represent an equal number of truly significant and stable platforms needed to sustain symbolic value creation according to different sets of consumer benefits and competitive scopes.

Among them, those brands that express a precise and authentic point of view inspiring consumer interests, opinions and attitudes and fuel their fame through positive word of mouth tend to me more successful in maintaining a premium price and extensions in several categories. These are brands that combine social benefits with their ability to extend to more than one category and target by going beyond their traditional core business: here are the so-called Lifestyle Brands. Previous research does not provide a model that identifies the key variables for the development of Lifestyle Brands nor one that explains the competencies and resources that fuel their success and longevity. In the next chapter we will focus on these types of brands and suggest a model that will attempt to address these issues.

3.4 BRAND EXTENSIONS: A TRUE OPPORTUNITY FOR JUST A FEW

The brands classification proposed in this chapter helps explain the ease or difficulty certain brands experience in entering new product categories that are relatively distant from their core business, as well as the long-term success or failure of these attempts. Semprini[4] argues that through extension strategies brands: (a) create products that are based on different 'know-hows'; (b) offer different benefits; (c) sometimes target different audiences than their traditional customers.

The different types of symbol intensive brands seem to be structurally more or less at ease in this activity. Theory tells us that success in a line or brand extension is based on two conditions:[5]

1. the more intangible the brand associations, the more distant the product categories open to brand extension; brands that are already perceived as Lifestyle are more likely to succeed in introducing new categories than product brands;
2. the closer the associations at product level the more distant the product categories open to brand extension. A brand may not have intangible association but still be able to succeed as there is a strong link between the core and the extended products.

By applying this approach to the universe of symbol intensive brands, we notice that Authority Brands are legitimated in extending into related categories by their 'hero' product or proprietary technology or know how, typically leading to a shift towards the category of Solution Brands. For example, the authority gained by Casio in electronic calculators, combined with the global spread of this product category, has certainly helped it achieve a leadership position in digital watches. But hardly ever can Authority Brands achieve uncorrelated brand extensions. A Cult Brand, while being admired in its own category for its original social benefits, can achieve line extensions but cannot always be successful in creating brand extensions. For example, when Harley-Davidson tried to offer clothing, lighters and perfumes, fans accused the company of jeopardising the brand, persuading the management to suspend any attempts to extend into inappropriate categories. Evidently, the masculine and very rugged values, although intangible, didn't fit with aftershaves and shampoo.

Not only does this raise the topic of intangibility of the associations for Cult Brands, but also introduces the aspect of product level similarity, meaning the alignment between the old and the new category. Icon Brands, and especially Icon Products, often have difficulty in extending into distant categories: think of the watch brands (Swatch) or spirits (Martini) that, although sometimes covering a wide territory in their core business, are unlikely to sustain significant non-correlated extensions. Starbucks has struggled so far to succeed in music or publishing because probably the brand is not perceived as relevant in those categories. On the other hand, Virgin managed to extend its brand across different businesses because its brand stands for forward thinking and value.

> **For symbol intensive brands**
> **extensions**
> **in other categories**
> **are not always a guaranteed**
> **success: some are**
> **at ease in approaching them, others risk**
> **diluting their integrity.**

When extensions are successful, as theory suggests, Iconic Brands leverage similarity on a product level, that is, a strong proximity in terms of features and benefits between core and extended categories: this is the case of Pirelli's 'Rubber Soul'. With the Pzero brand, Pirelli attempt to combine fashion and technology by applying industrial design codes to sneakers and selected outwear and accessories.[6] Or think of the Caterpillar brand with its earthmoving machines, successfully entering work wear apparel.

When on the other hand it is a particular philosophy or vision that supports the extension to other categories (instead of it being a product expertise), we see interesting phenomena. For example, the diverse portfolio of activities in which Virgin operates, the success of Diesel and Ralph Lauren in the clothing, accessories, perfumes and home collection categories, or the case of Chanel, which brings a unique and original point of view not only in fashion and accessories, but also in perfumes, cosmetics and more recently in the jewellery and watchmaking industries.

The subject alone would justify a further line of research, but it can generally be concluded that all these success case studies have resisted the temptation to grant licences to make money, invading the market with generic products, often only vaguely inspired by the brand stylistic codes, or just characterised by their logo.

This is common practice in the world of fashion brands and brands that define themselves as 'lifestyle'. It can lead to positive economic results in the short term, when the brand is cool, but if not carefully managed can undermine the brand equity and therefore the sustainability of the same core business in the long run.

4

HOW LIFESTYLE BRANDS WORK:
AN INTERPRETATIVE MODEL

4.1 LIFESTYLES AND LIFESTYLE BRANDS

In looking more closely at the Lifestyle Brands category, it is necessary to start questioning the term 'lifestyle' itself, a often misused term. The use of lifestyles as an analytical construct dates back to the famous text by Thorstein Veblen's *The Theory of the Leisure Class* (1994 [1899]) and Max Weber's studies on the concept of status. The term has since been widely used and diffused by Alfred Adler, an Austrian physician and founder of the school of individual psychology. According to Adler, each individual has his or her own unique and inimitable lifestyle with which he/she approaches the world and interprets with originality.[1]

According to other scholars, the term 'lifestyle' refers to aspects of cultural trends as well as aspects of value that are strongly associated with consumption. In the United States, Bell,[2] Rainwater, Coleman and Handel,[3] Havighurst and Feigenbaum[4] were the first to talk about lifestyles by studying purchasing behaviour. Today, research into lifestyles represents a crossroad of different disciplines, from sociology to medicine to social sciences. However, the original German word (*Lebensstil*) originally used in sociology with a precise meaning, is now trivialised and is used in

58

multiple contexts: there are lifestyles in health, nutrition, fashion, cosmetics, furniture and leisure. In reality, 'lifestyle' is a systemic concept, and in order to decode it, it is necessary to combine three dimensions:

- the social status of the person (defined as 'class' by some authors, e.g. Bourdieu);
- its attitudes and preferences;
- its behaviour (or praxis, according to Bourdieu).

Social class therefore is not enough to define homogenous lifestyles. Among affluent consumers in fact we find segments that differ with their purchasing and consumer behaviour patterns. Some love to flaunt, others seek pleasure and self-gratification, and others, despite the possibilities, exhibit a frugal behaviour oriented towards mass-produced or discounted products. As noted above, the term 'lifestyle' nowadays suggests a model in which people associate patterns of relationships, behaviour and consumption. The simplest and most immediate definition to be used in management perhaps is still the one that dates back to the 1970s: lifestyles, and therefore styles of consumption, reflect a person's attitudes, interests and opinions. As described by Plummer,[5] attitudes refer to how individuals spend their time and money; interests reflect the things that people consider important at present; and opinions reflect how people feel about themselves and world around them.

By adopting this meaning, the concept has been increasingly used as a basis for explaining postmodern consumption. There are those who have observed how 'lifestyles' have overtaken classes, education and gender in becoming a main criterion for segmenting social groups typical of advanced industrial societies, revealing the stratification and sociocultural diversity.[6]

When you move from lifestyle to Lifestyle Brands, what is an already difficult concept to define becomes even more elusive and ambiguous. Today many companies, from clothing design to travel, use the term 'lifestyle', believing that through their own products they are promoting a certain way of life. Actually, the term is often used by these brands only as an indicator of the product range: those who sell shoes, apparel and fragrances consider themselves to be selling a lifestyle as opposed to those solely specialising in and focused on footwear.

> **Lifestyle Brands describe who we are,**
> **what we believe, what tribe we belong to.**
> **They communicate our status and our aspirations.**
> **They indicate the way we deal with our life**
> **and sometimes reflect our own unconscious.**

In truth, a 'Lifestyle Brand' status isn't just achieved by way of a wide product range but above all, as seen in Chapter 3, by the type of benefit and symbolic value that the customer associates with the brand. Starting with the idea that consumers are increasingly adopting brands to express their identities, some recent contributions have defined Lifestyle Brands as one of the possible ways of consumer self-expression.[7] According to other authors, Lifestyle Brands possess the following attributes:

- a product with benefits related to self-expression;
- an integrated communications strategy;
- a brand based on several product lines.

In our opinion, as detailed in the following section, it is not from the product but from the brand that benefits start arising, by expressing the values and aspirations of a social group or culture. Secondly, it is not only communication that can express the brand vision and beliefs, building a unique and holistic experience. Finally, we share the thought that a Lifestyle Brand, more than others, can be successfully extended to several categories.

According to our approach, a brand becomes a Lifestyle Brand when it promotes social benefits through a point of view on the world that a significant number of people adhere to by becoming customers, because they are represented in terms of attitudes, opinions and interests.

The questions we ask ourselves at this point are: how is a Lifestyle Brands created and how does it work? What are its key elements and where does it derive its value from? How can you maintain its success over time? Lifestyle Brands deserve more careful observation.

4.2 AN INTERPRETATIVE MODEL

Great brands are simple and direct, and so are Lifestyle Brands. The core mechanism of Lifestyle Brands therefore is based on a simple premise: in order to represent the attitudes, opinions and interests of a group of individuals the brand must first and foremost have a clear, original and coherent point of view. This view has to:

- be based on socially relevant values, expressed though an interesting and authentic storytelling;
- be explained through a distinctive and distinguishing manifesto that goes beyond the classical brand positioning and a simple value proposition;
- be expressed in a recognisable and consistent manner across all consumer/brand touch points.

We found out that what the brand believes in, how the brand states it, and the way it expresses it are the three cornerstones of a successful Lifestyle Brand (Figure 4.1).

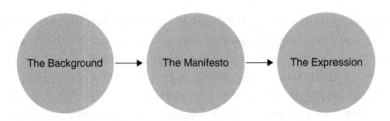

Figure 4.1   **The Lifestyle Brands cornerstones**

Therefore we propose a model consisting of three simple elements that summarise what we have observed both in the academic literature and in benchmarking business cases:

- the Background;
- the Manifesto;
- the Expression.

It is important to notice that the three cornerstones of a Lifestyle Brand are not exclusive to them. Some of the components of the Background, the Manifesto and the Expression have already been discussed in academic research and may be present in other types of symbol intensive brands, Icon and Cult in particular. However, only in Lifestyle Brands do all three components work in harmony, drawing from this their unique value.

4.2.1   The Background

The Background of a Lifestyle Brand includes both its Credo and series of stories capable of involving its 'followers', fuelling the desirability and the brand mythology.

Credo is a Latin word indicating a set of fundamental beliefs or a guiding principle. It is a founding element of any strategic thinking for a Lifestyle Brand. The Credo is represented by a few simple, fundamental attributes that describe the unique and original perspective the brand has of the world. More precisely, it identifies the pillars on which the brand's ideal world should be based, laying the foundations of the brand ideology. For example, the adidas Originals Credo consists of Originality, Authenticity and Creativity, summarised in the call to action 'Celebrate Originality'. For Gucci, it's about Seduction, Power and Self-realisation while for Volcom it's 'Athlete-driven, Innovative and Creative'.

The Credo tends to be characterised by aspirational values, but at the same time is precise enough to guide attitudes, behaviours and decisions throughout the organisation. Virgin claims not to have substantially changed its Credo in the past forty years, having always interpreted it not as an abstract declaration but as a reflection of its genuine way of doing business. By embodying the values of Fun, a healthy sense of Competition and Challenge, Sir Richard Branson observes in his biography: 'Every minute of every day should be lived as wholeheartedly as possible.'

In describing the Credo, the fewer and more 'to the point' the words are, the easier it is to guide the organisation by inspiring and influencing small everyday decisions as well as major strategic ones, such as commitment to Science, Community and Service for the American cosmetic brand Kiehl's.

The other key component of the Background are the Stories that can be told about the company, its products, its customers/users, its founder, its place of origin, its businesses, its innovations and so on. The Stories can be seen as a practical and concrete reflection of the Credo.

**Great symbol intensive
brands are like stories.**

All successful Lifestyle Brands and many of those that used to be Lifestyle and have now become Icons, are a treasure trove of anecdotes, starting from the biography of the founder up to his/her memorable undertakings. Chanel, one of the first Lifestyle Brands, and today an Icon, has long been an inspiring way of life for its customers. The very life of Mademoiselle Coco has been marked by true milestones for the empowerment of women, from haircuts to the introduction of trousers in womenswear, to her attitude towards marriage. Her Parisian home-studio in Rue Cambon is still a place of pilgrimage.

The rows of bare-chested models, the loud music, the dancing shop assistants, the scent, the controversial and provocative stances in the media have fuelled for years the myth of Abercrombie & Fitch. Stories that revolve around the origins of Nike, the swoosh and its legendary founder continue to captivate millions of fans around the world. The founder in fact was Philip Hampson Knight: innovative, controversial, immensely successful, and the most powerful businessman in the business of sports, according to *Sporting News*. And what to say about the 'Just Do It' campaign, considered by *Ad Age* magazine as one of the best advertising slogans of the twentieth century, or the heroic deeds of Michael Jordan or Tiger Woods, both sponsored by the iconic brand?

One could go on for pages, compiling a rich collection of anecdotes for dozens of brands. But these Stories should not be simply recorded, or just be a historical reconstruction of the past, for one simple reason: if I ask a brand to represent me, this brand should evoke a rich, interesting and engaging world, at least for me and for those like me. Stories must be memorable, be able to emotionally involve the brand aficionados and encourage them to share the Stories with other individuals with similar interests. They need to be Stories that have the power to spread virally,

Stories that you want to speak of to people to whom you feel close.

4.2.2   The Manifesto

If a Lifestyle Brand wants to represent an individual or a group of individuals, it needs to propose a distinctive and original perspective on the world and make it immediately recognisable through some codes that represent it. These two components constitute the Manifesto of the brand and can be defined as the Lifestyle Proposition and the Lifestyle Code respectively.

The Manifesto, as a public declaration of principles and intentions, is something different from the Vision and Mission. The Vision describes the purpose, the reason for existence and the ultimate goal of an organisation. The Mission materialises the Vision into a concrete goal. For example, if Nike's Vision is: 'to bring inspiration and innovation to every athlete in the world', its Mission is 'Crush adidas'. Nike will have achieved its Vision the moment it has beaten adidas. This is very different from the famous swoosh and the 'Just Do It' call to action in which the aficionados will recognise the brand, and which summarises the proposed lifestyle.

Lifestyle Proposition

The Lifestyle Proposition is not a doctrine but a set of intentions and topics, which generally originate from the Visionary Leader who established the brand, eventually becoming very important for those who share his own feeling. Volcom has a 'brandifesto' declaring that the company was founded on liberation, innovation and experimentation while remaining dedicated to the breakdown of established traditions. Volcom's Lifestyle Proposition embodies the free and creative spirit of youth culture, addressing kids who share the same passion for art, music, movies, skateboarding, surfing, snowboarding and motocross. The brand supports athletes, artists and musicians by providing a platform through which people can express themselves and share these passions together. This collaborative effort can be seen in projects like 'Let the Kids Ride Free', the surf competition 'Volcom Pipeline Pro' or the record label Volcom Entertainment.

> **In Lifestyle Brands, product quality and symbolic meaning are closely related.**

Similarly, as stated by Ben Pruess, who led the adidas Originals line's success: 'We have become part of hip-hop, skateboarding, and high-fashion simply by being adopted by these communities. And we want to continue to do so.' Renzo Rosso, the founder of Diesel, goes even further by proclaiming: 'Diesel is not aimed at youth culture, youth culture is Diesel.' So that the public can decide whether to buy in or not, the Lifestyle Proposition must be clear and unambiguous, and ultimately discriminatory. Lifestyle Brands are not made to please everyone, but to be adored only by those who recognise themselves in the Proposition and intend to join. And this is one of the secrets of their success: the ability to be discriminating. As Mike Jeffries, CEO of Abercrombie & Fitch, said:

> *In every school there are the cool and popular kids, and then there are the not-so-cool kids. Candidly, we go after the cool kids. We go after the attractive all-American kid with a great attitude and a lot of friends. A lot*

of people don't belong [in our clothes], and they can't belong. Are we exclusionary? Absolutely. Those companies that are in trouble are trying to target everybody: young, old, fat, skinny. But then you become totally vanilla. You don't alienate anybody, but you don't excite anybody, either

Obviously the Lifestyle Proposition must be based on the brand Credo and should constantly find a confirmation in the facts, stories and anecdotes that represent the brand mythology. But while it is often not hard to find stories and anecdotes about the brand, or at least that build up to the Credo, it is almost impossible to find an explicit description of the Lifestyle Proposition in corporate documents or annual reports. For example, one can infer Virgin's Lifestyle Proposition from the words of Sir Richard Branson when he describes the origin of his group:[8]

I realized that there was a huge market out there for value-for-money-based products other than music. No one likes to be ripped off and a lack of competition is bad for consumers. So it was simply the realization that if we offer a more affordable, fun and good-quality product, people would buy it. And we've made that simple philosophy work with everything from trains and planes, to mobile phones, wedding dresses and condoms.

Doing good, having fun and making a difference is the focus of Virgin's Lifestyle Proposition. Based on this, Virgin has gone against the rules of the big multinational corporations by offering products and services characterised by a fun and liberating but not oppressive attitude, keeping itself tuned with 'real' people, and especially youth.

The Lifestyle Proposition must continually understand the lifestyle evolution in terms of interests, opinions and attitudes in order to stay relevant for its audience. Even if it does not yet seem entirely supported by facts, Virgin's Lifestyle Proposition has recently become more a concrete thought, widening to aspects such as eco-sustainability and the pursuit of individual happiness:

> *As global citizens we want to provide people with products and services that will help them to embrace a more sustainable lifestyle. Our lifestyle not only impacts others but also the planet. Living a more 'sustainable lifestyle' is about making more responsible choices. So far, a sustainable lifestyle has been associated with sacrifice or compromise, giving up the choice and freedom we currently enjoy. Virgin's vision is the opposite of this. We believe that living sustainably doesn't have to mean cutting back or frugality, and responsibility shouldn't be dull or difficult.*

While most of the time the Lifestyle Proposition is clear in the mind of the leader, it is seldom shared in a formal way within the organisation. Often the discriminating factor between what is considered on-brand, therefore adhering to the lifestyle offered by the brand, or off-brand, is located mainly in the emotional reactions of the leader himself. As journalist Benoit Denizet-Lewis observes in a detailed profile of Abercrombie & Fitch and its founder Mike Jeffries:

> *Jeffries says that A&F is a collaborative environment, but in the end he makes every decision – from the hiring of the models to the placement of every item of clothing in every*

> *store. There are model stores for each of the four brands at A&F headquarters, and he spends much of his time making sure they're perfect. When they are, everything is photographed and sent to individual outlets to be replicated to the last detail.*

This is a common practice for many fashion companies and designers. The Lifestyle Proposition must be patiently inferred from a careful analysis of the available material and interviews, and be thoroughly validated with the leader. The same Benoit Denizet-Lewis reconstructs Abercrombie & Fitch's Lifestyle Proposition in the US of the 1990s:

> *Much more than just a brand, Abercrombie & Fitch successfully resuscitated a 1990s version of a 1950s ideal – the white, masculine 'beefcake' – during a time of political correctness and rejection of '50s orthodoxy. But it did so with profound and significant differences. A&F aged the masculine ideal downward, celebrating young men in their teens and early 20s with smooth, gym-toned bodies and perfectly coifed hair. [...]. For many young men, to wear Abercrombie is to broadcast masculinity, athleticism and inclusion in the 'cool boys club' without even having to open their mouths.*

The aspiration or identification in a Lifestyle Proposition should then allow the individual to better express his/her personality, or at least one side of it. In fact, a rich and multifaceted personality, which sometimes can even combine opposites, is one of the characteristics of today's consumer. The same person can be a strict manager by day, an aggressive biker in the evening, a sophisticated weekend sailor, and much more. In virtually every case, there will be a brand that will help to transfer these traits of an individual's personality, sometimes even combining different references to them in the same outfit.

Lifestyle Codes

Typically, successful Lifestyle Brands are instantly recognisable. 'If you say something is "very Ralph Lauren", you're immediately understood,' said Audrey Hepburn in 1992 at the CFDA Lifetime Achievement Award Ceremony.

More specifically, Lifestyle Brands acquire some characteristic codes that become permanent signs communicating a particular point of view of the world. We call this Lifestyle Codes. These signs may include logos, shapes, patterns, materials, colours, details or even specific types of product. For example, Prada's 'dignified' nylon has established itself as an unmistakable symbol of innovative and sophisticated functionality on top of representing Prada's take on fashion.

Burberry's tartan design symbolises the Brit chic spirit of the brand. Kiehl's packaging defies convention in the premium cosmetics segment: bottles of white plastic with complex labels that explain the brand's focus on ingredients, thus expressing substance over form. Lifestyle Codes, as we shall see, influences the expression of the brand, but in turn the Codes are influenced: new products, campaigns or brand behaviours may be particularly successful and become iconic, thus joining the brand's characteristic set of Codes. It is important, however, to distinguish when this happens or doesn't: by definition Codes must remain few in number.

Camper shoes are not only extremely comfortable but are a reflection of the Mediterranean and especially of Spanish lifestyle, which is expressed in the brand's call to action: 'Walk, Don't Run'. The playfulness, vibrancy and colour associated with the brand are present at every level of its expression: in stores, products and communication.

Brands are cultural entities, engines that live in time and space. Therefore, symbols change their meaning across countries and cultures, just as feelings and values do. This is true not only for the codes and signals of a sexual or religious group, which is an obvious fact, but also for seemingly innocuous ones, such as numbers and colours.

In fact, the culture of origin of Lifestyle Brands is the basis of their system of values, and determines the Manifesto. For example, in its first collections, Victoria's Secret purposely evoked the English upper-class style, just as Louis Vuitton continues to evoke the opulent tradition of French aristocracy or Uniqlo recalls Japanese Zen and manga cartoons. In these cases the customer must be culturally equipped to understand the message. But it is also true that there are some generational transfers that are common to most countries and cultures: for example, all women want to be the most beautiful, all young people are to a certain extent 'against the establishment' and, at a certain age, all want to feel young and fit, and try to find codes that express these needs.

4.2.3 The Expression

The Brand Manifesto becomes tangible through communication activities, direct interaction with the consumer, especially in-store, and though its products or services. These three components are the expression of the brand. Especially for products with a high symbolic content, the expression has increasingly moved towards the construction of a holistic experience across all touch points and relationships with the customer. A brand like Ralph Lauren, which bears values of refined elegance, typical of an 'East Coast' American culture, has built stores that reproduce the environment of an American upper-class home, communicated with campaigns showing beautiful young and elegant people, and offered iconic yet updated products that recall the colours, materials and styles of American casual-chic campuses. The critical success factors for Lifestyle Brands are consistency and authenticity, since the acceptance of a proposed way of life is based on a critical evaluation of real-life experiences, at all levels.

Expression in communication

If for consumer goods communication is often structured around a copy strategy that expresses the product or brand attributes and benefits, communications for a Lifestyle Brand focus on the correct representation of the Lifestyle Proposition by using a highly aspirational language, generally based on image aesthetics. It uses little or no copy, is understandable without the need for translations, and often uses known testimonials that are relevant to the target.

Implicit motivations and symbolic elements, which are more easily conceptualised and understood via a image-based communication, tend to prevail for Lifestyle Brands over functional attributes. In this regard, it is fascinating to note the difference between the iPod launch advertising campaign and that of any other MP3 player. Apple's dancing silhouettes did not need copy and the campaign was understood cross-culturally. Moreover, unlike for consumer goods, where communication is primarily (but increasingly not only) the art of persuasion, communication for Lifestyle Brands is primarily the art of storytelling and inspiration.

Speaking of movies, Casetti and Di Chio[9] define narrative as 'a chain of situations in which events take place, where characters operate immersed in specific environments'. Similarly, communication of a Lifestyle Brand should comprise of a dynamic combination of characters, events and environments, tied together by situations that have the power to affect the target of the communication as well as fuel the authenticity of the brand. If narration is a tool needed to build authenticity, differentiation and word of mouth, the book Made to Stick by Chip and Dan Heath[10] offers a simple recipe to make a subject become memorable and convincing. It is summarised in the acronym SUCCES: the story must be Simple, Unexpected, Concrete, Credible, Emotional, and full of anecdotes (Stories).

A good example is Patagonia: in 1990 their 'Field Reports' about nature, expressed through the experiences and words of many athletes, travellers and adventurers, have been an opportunity to describe the brand. These 'Ambassadors' are not athletes but are actually spokespeople and experimenters of the brand.

Narrative today can take advantage of a variety of channels. This is according to the most advanced approach called 'cross media storytelling'[11] and engages consumers through different means, shifting from the traditional linear story, to a more complex, multi-dimensional plot with a unifying idea where new media represents a great opportunity to stage the views of the brand. Burberry has introduced an approach for involvement and narrative that uses a series of web-based tools, such as Burberry Acoustic or Art of the Trench. Burberry Acoustic is a form of collaboration with some of the most promising talents of the British music scene, selected directly by the Chief Creative Officer Christopher Bailey. These artists record unique acoustic sessions that are then made available to the brands' broad and global audience. Art of the Trench is a user-generated social media project by Scott Schuman, the founder of the blog 'The Sartorialist', where customers share their images in which they are wearing the famous trench coats.

A timeless and iconic product quickly becomes contemporary and part of a narrative. For brands that want to activate and carry on a conversation with their communities of customers, it has become necessary nowadays to generate initiatives and turn to stable resources to properly manage social media. Adidas originals ensures its relationship with teens with a continuous flow of digital content that invites them to stay connected to the brand 365 days a year. In this regard, the CEO of adidas sport style division, Herman Deininger, explained:

> *after observing the way our customers use media, and having the ability to use interactive tools to stay in touch with them, it was easy to decide to focus our efforts on digital media and to bring our campaign 'Celebrate Originality' to life in our stores.*

Lifestyle Brands use storytelling indifferently off and on line to engage their clientele. Tiffany & Co., for example, deployed a micro-site called 'What Makes Love True' to sell an online narrative to go along with the rings. Passion and involvement are essential to establish an emotional bond with the consumer, without which the same Lifestyle Brand (or aspiring one) would have no reason to exist. This can be achieved only through a direct interaction with the consumer, be it virtual or physical, such as the point of sale.

Expression trough interactions

If in some sectors, such as music or books, the digitisation of the product is contributing to the disappearance of traditional distribution, Lifestyle Brands products are almost always material and difficult to virtualise, maintaining the importance of a physical distribution and direct interaction with the consumer. The store is key from two points of view:

- from a consumer point of view for the necessity to fully perceive the Lifestyle Proposition, interact with the brand, meet peers and access new products;
- from a brand point of view for the essential role the sales assistants have in the narrative, through the description of product characteristics and the dissemination of stories and anecdotes that have the power to capture the consumer's attention and emotional involvement.

For many Lifestyle Brands the store is like a portal, a venue for communities of aficionados, where one experiences, gathers ideas and continues the conversation about the brand. Kiehl's built its brand experience by also incorporating the attitude of sales staff – strictly dressed in white, like the product packaging – they welcome, listen, know products and resolve problems. The policy of handing out samples to the customer is part of the generosity with which the brand behaves.

In the US, after having launched the trend of having huge and expensive flagship stores like Niketown, Nike has more recently decided to focus on customer relationships by reducing the size of its stores and changing the content of the experience towards the direction of a greater management of its community of fans. Customers interested in running can register for the Nike+ Run Club, view calendars of events in the area, get advice on training and test new models of shoes. A greater attention was also given to the brand's Credo and Stories, with initiatives such as artistic interpretations of co-founder Bill Bowerman's face, reproductions of the Waffle iron or an Air Jordan gallery.

Direct distribution is still the preferred channel to fully express the Manifesto for a Lifestyle Brand. However, given the need to 'live' and 'let live' the brand to its customers, multi-brand distribution instead poses major problems of management and control, except for particular types of licensed products such as sunglasses or perfume. Even though it still conveys the brand's Manifesto, the digital channel will never be able to completely replace the physical distribution because of the need to create a human relationship with those who want to join the Lifestyle Proposition.

Expression through the product

The brand/customer relationship finds its peak with the product experience, but also results from the physical interaction the consumer has with the product itself. According to Hekkert, product experience is divided into three levels: aesthetic pleasure, attribution of meaning, and emotional response. Hekkert defines product experience as:

> the entire set of affects that is elicited by the interaction between a user and a product, including the degree to which all our senses are gratified (aesthetic experience), the meanings we attach to the product (experience of meaning) and the feelings and emotions that are elicited (emotional experience).[12]

Although often confused with being present solely at a visual level, aesthetic experience has a specific relevance on auditory, tactile and kinaesthetic experiences as well. The sound of a car door that closes, the softness of a fabric, the shape of an object includes, for example, the aesthetic experience of the product.

The semantic level of experience concerns our ability to assign symbolic meanings and values to a product. Through cognitive processes such as memory, interpretation and association, we can give a sense to the product experience. The car door that closes with a smooth, firm, muffled sound, for example, can communicate a sense of preciseness and robustness. A fabric that is very soft to touch can evoke quality, comfort and warmth. But clearly these cognitive processes largely depend on both individual and cultural differences: the same aesthetic experience can lead to very different meanings to different people and groups. Finally, the emotional experience concerns the emotions evoked by the interaction with a product. Using the same example, a car door that closes with a smooth, firm and muffled sound, which communicates a sense of preciseness and robustness, can then lead to emotions such as feeling of safety and contentment. Love, attraction, desire, pride or pleasure are other examples of emotions that can be evoked by the experience of the product. Once again in this case, behind an emotion there is the meaning that each of us attaches to the experience.

As observed by Desmet and Hekkert, although these three levels of product experience can be separated quite clearly conceptually, they are in fact closely interrelated and often difficult to isolate in daily practical experience. They are also experiences that are always influenced by the context in which they occur, which means that potential control on the actual Product Experience (and therefore the brand perception) is limited.

Returning to our model, it is essential that the brand expression is consistent with the Credo, conveys the Lifestyle Proposition, helps build new Stories and expresses characteristic codes of the brand in a seamless and consistent way, both on and off-line.

4.3 THE 'HUMAN FACTOR'

One might ask why some brands never come to be fully adopted by a significant group of consumers while others

Figure 4.2 **A model for Lifestyle Brands**

are capable of representing a group of individuals in a relatively natural and profound way; or why certain brands reach this level but cannot maintain their status over time.

The answer is mainly in the human factor that drives and animates these brands. Visionary Leadership is initially essential to create the necessary disruption to break market rules and gather around the brand an initial group of 'followers'. Subsequently you need an organisation of supporters that shares, keeps alive and develops the same principles by giving structure to the original intuition and helping to translate it into products, communication and experience year after year, even in different categories, and in all markets of the world. The human factor is what makes the model a dynamic one, and may explain the success or decline over time of a symbol intensive brand, and in particular of a Lifestyle Brand (Figure 4.2).

4.3.1 Visionary Leaders

To understand symbol intensive brands we have to see them as generating symbols rather than producing physical products. This is the role in which a Visionary Leader makes the difference: he/she may be purely a creative, as in the case of Miuccia Prada, or have a more entrepreneurial mind, as Steve Jobs, Enzo Ferrari and Renzo Rosso. Or, he/she might be a great combination of the two, such as Giorgio Armani and Ralph Lauren. He/she can start individually or belong to an organisation, like Alec Issigonis, who designed the first Mini in 1959. In any case, a Visionary Leader is an individual with a charismatic profile, a higher sensitivity and a strongly assertive and original perspective that he/she is able to express through a product and a brand. Over time this brand will prove to be able to interpret, express and amplify the ethos and the social identity of a significant group of people.

Typically, Visionary Leaders:

- are in tune with the current social situation and with the transformations taking place in the context in which they live;
- embed their activity within their daily lives, influencing it with their commitment and a critical sense of affinity;
- are vital, receptive, in constant tension between the imaginary and the concrete, constantly evolving and searching for the meaning of existence and the world, but at the same time driven by a never-ending tendency to experiment;
- are brave.

The most visionary of them are motivated by a deep desire to give a voice to their era, distilling their role and their personalities in the products themselves, which in turn become points of reference. When Coco Chanel said 'Women should dress for themselves, not for their men,' she wanted to develop not only women's fashion but also the actual conditions of women in society. The mass production of luxury was sensed by Pierre Cardin: 'I asked myself: why should only the rich be able to afford exclusive fashion, why not the man and woman on the street as well? I can change that! And I did.' Giorgio Armani based his entire stylistic research on the evolution of gender roles in modern Western society, stating: 'I eliminate the differences between men and women.' Behind the famous phrase 'Starbucks represents something beyond a cup of coffee', there is actually the original vision of Howard Schultz, its CEO:[13]

> *we had a vision, to create an atmosphere in our stores that drew people in and gave them a sense of wonder and romance in the midst of their harried lives. We had an idealistic dream, that our company could be far more than the paradigm defined by corporate America in the past.*

But the role of the Visionary Leader does not end at the first claim of a product or brand. Especially in the case of Lifestyle Brands, the Visionary Leader is necessary to personify and represent the brand Credo, to create stories and anecdotes that can continuously feed into the brand mythology and to maintain the Brand Manifesto as authentic and relevant over time. The latter is the most rare and difficult thing to accomplish.

The original vision behind the brand tends to weaken for several reasons: it can be copied or developed by competitors, it can lose its characteristics of being current and new, or simply because the social context that created the conditions for the magical chemistry between the brand and its fans changes. There are very few brands that have managed to reinvent themselves and be able to represent the profound identity of groups of individuals across generations. Those who succeeded did so thanks to their leaders who reinvented their vision over time, as Steve Jobs did with Apple, or by using different Visionary Leaders in different eras as in the case of Ferrari, where Luca di Montezemolo was able to take on this role after the death of the founder, while maintaining a high symbolic value of the brand.

In many other cases the original intuition of the Visionary Leader was not renewed, revitalised or replaced, making the brand simply become an Icon or generally a brand of prestige. It might still be able to produce good economic results, but it is not essential any more for its group of 'followers', becoming increasingly dependent on fashions, on economic trends and on the success of individual collections or product lines. Or, more simply, it gradually disappears after the death of its Visionary Leader.

4.3.2 Organisational mechanisms

As mentioned in the beginning, however, the existence of a Visionary Leader is necessary for a Lifestyle Brand but is not always sufficient to ensure a long-lasting and success-ful existence. One person (or more likely a small group of people) is needed to transform the Brand Manifesto into a reality by designing and building day after day not just the product/service but also the communication and the ways of interacting with the consumer.

An Operational Leader, or a front line that is perfectly in tune with the Visionary Leader, is the transmission belt between theory and practice, between the wording of the Manifesto and its translation into reality. Often the fail-ure to achieve the full potential of a Lifestyle Brand lies in the weakness or lack of this feature, which translates into communication, products and experiences that are inconsistent with the Lifestyle Proposition and with those iconic characteristic signs that make the brand unique and instantly recognisable.

> **The secret of successful Lifestyle Brands
> is the internal and external alignment
> to the Lifestyle Proposition.**

Some of the most successful Lifestyle Brands, and some of the brands that come close to this status, activate a series of organisational mechanisms to acquire and maintain resources that are in line with the Brand Credo, ensuring that any activity helps express and give substance to the Manifesto. Howard Schultz, CEO of Starbucks, said: 'When I looked back, I realized we fashioned a brand in a way that no business school textbook could have ever prescribed. We built the brand first with our people, not with consumers. That's the secret power of the Starbucks brand: the personal attachment our partners feel and the connection they make with our customers.'

He is echoed by Sir Richard Branson, founder and CEO of Virgin: 'We have always believed that to create a strong brand, you must first create a strong culture that supports it.'

In practice, this means to:

- think more in terms of competencies and strategy and not just profits. In other words, acquire and develop resources and skills within the company that are more in tune with the Lifestyle Proposition;
- use these resources and skills to build a customer experience consistent with the Manifesto;
- create new ways to keep the brand narrative alive both inside and outside the organisation.

Many Lifestyle Brands use creative tools for staff selection to ensure they attract and hire the right people. Some, such as Nike, clearly state the brand Credo directly on their website or in personnel search websites;[14] others, such as Patagonia, are also focused on the personal interests of the people they hire.[15]

But other types of symbol intensive brands such as the Authority or Icon Brands invest more and more on candidate profiling. By testing the candidate's creative resources and problem-solving skills, Google manages to select profiles from more than 1,300 CVs it receives each day. They once even published an ad anonymously in the form of a mathematical problem, by means of posters displayed in Silicon Valley. Only after having solved a number of steps did the candidates find out the author was Google. Once joining the company, newcomers are immediately 'baptised'. In their first week of work, the so-called "nooglers" attend the traditional weekly meeting with the senior team. They must, however, sit in a separate section, wear the colourful 'nooglers' cap and wear a sign with a series of personal information to make fun of themselves and be made fun of. When the company was still of limited size, the founders were present at each meeting, and the presentation of each 'noogler' was greeted by an applause, giving start to real on-boarding activities. Google is known for its low personnel turnover.

Other brands such as Virgin and Starbucks have developed toolkits, manuals and guides on the brand's philosophy and values, as well as assigning tutorship and support for newcomers.

Starbucks plans the arrival of a new manager weeks in advance, assembling an 'Immersion Team' composed of colleagues and partners who will be responsible for the newcomer's ability to express the 'Starbucks Experience' in the shortest possible time, providing materials, contacts and information on rules and procedures.

> **New hires must
> live the brand experience.**

A contact person, the 'Immersion Buddy', has the task of giving immediate feedback and guiding the learning of the new arrival. The actual process consists of three phases: the first in which the newcomer, regardless of the position and status, directly works in a store to experience first hand the creation of the customer experience; a second where he/she meets some of the key people to better understand the procedures and best practices related to his/her function; and a third devoted to investigating his/her specific role. The Brand Credo and the basic principles of behaviour are included in the Green Apron Book that is distributed to every employee.

Virgin also has a toolkit for new employees, but, true to its philosophy, it is the only formal element of its on-boarding process. The Brand Credo is clearly articulated upfront, but everyone is then asked to interpret it according to their own sensibility. In particular, managers must devise appropriate ways to keep the brand philosophy alive with their respective teams. The toolkit contains guidelines, metrics and tools to understand what is on or off-brand and facilitate decision-making on an individual basis.

Finally, many instruments also exist to keep the brand narrative alive within the organisation.

For example, Zappos, a leader in online distribution of clothing and footwear in the US, asked its own employees to write the Company Culture Book, bringing together thoughts, ideas and anecdotes related to events experienced with colleagues or clients.

Virgin, once again strengthens the cohesion of its communities through internal communication activities, the first-hand exposure of its Visionary Leader and the celebration of merits and achievements. Sir Richard Branson in person reads each observation and suggestion received from the staff. In two separate weekends during summer, more than 30,000 people (staff and their families) attend a party at Branson's residence in Oxfordshire.

Both customers and colleagues can nominate excellent employees, allowing them to access specific incentive programs such as Virgin Atlantic's or Virgin Holidays' Heroes, Virgin Mobile's Shout Scheme, the Virgin Money's Academy Awards and the coveted 'Star of the Year' open to all employees of the group.

In the past some critics showed scepticism about the return on investment for this kind of activity, but those who did probably ignored the importance of building a superior employee brand experience. In the 1990s, a group of Harvard researchers[16] demonstrated through the Service-Profit Chain model that there is a direct link between experiences of superior quality, customer loyalty and financial performance, in terms of growth and profit. Although this approach has subsequently been discussed and further developed, it is now believed that building an employee experience around the corporate culture can contribute to about 20 per cent of the Total Shareholder Return of an organisation, certainly an underestimated value for those brands we have defined in this book as Lifestyle Brands.

4.4 A MODEL FOR LIFESTYLE BRANDS, BUT NOT ONLY ...

As we mentioned at the beginning of this chapter, the elements that make up a Lifestyle Brand are not solely exclusive to them, but are found in many of the brands that we have defined as symbol intensive. However, all these components are present simultaneously only in Lifestyle Brands, where they form a system in which each plays a clear role in relation to the other. We will try to describe this status with the cases presented in the next chapter.

Almost all symbol intensive brands have Stories that can captivate people who feel more close to them, although Authority Brands will most likely feature anecdotes related to the characteristics, performance or the unique style of the product. Not all symbol intensive brands are based on a Credo: for example, a Potential Fad can achieve its goal through its ability to grasp the tendency of the moment. While over time it may become an Icon Brand, it will not necessarily need to explain a clear and coherent set of values (although this step is likely to happen). The same Icon Brand will almost certainly have particularly evident stylistic codes or aesthetic characteristics without it having to be a Lifestyle Brand. Similarly, a brand does not necessarily need to be Lifestyle in to express itself in distinctive and relevant forms of communication and interaction with customers: it can leverage substantially similar organisational mechanisms.

Generally, this model can provide guidance on how to maximise the economic return of all symbol intensive brands.

Finally, behind a symbol intensive brand there is almost always a leader of extraordinary capabilities. These capabilities, however, differ according to the various brand typologies: someone with technical skills for an Authority Brand, great management skills for a Solution Brand, creative and marketing skills in the case of an Icon Brand or Potential Fad. And a passionate and charismatic leader is often behind a Cult Brand. We can conclude that the unique features and characteristics of a Lifestyle Brand are twofold: the presence of a Visionary Leader and his ability to express and articulate a Lifestyle Proposition. These are the two elements without which you would not be able to create that alchemy that allows a brand to inspire, guide and clearly indicate a direction to people.

5

THE MODEL IN ACTION

5.1 A FEW EMBLEMATIC CASES

In selecting some specific cases to illustrate this model we came across Authority Brands such as Loro Piana, Cult Brands such as Ferrari and Ducati, and Iconic Brands such as Tiffany and Chanel. We found brands that used to be an Authority, Icon or Cult but have gradually shifted to something else, sometimes becoming Solution Brands, such as Timberland and Lacoste, at the price perhaps of a certain dilution of the original idea in order to cover a larger number of categories. We also found some brands that had been legendary for someone or somewhere in the world but today have simply disappeared.

Our aim was, however, to study cases of brands able to deliver social benefits for a relatively large number of individuals and serve multiple market segments: those brands that in the previous chapters we have defined as Lifestyle Brands. In this context we have encountered brands that used to be powerful but no longer are, such as The Body Shop, which has definitely been a positive force for environmental awareness for millions of people through its presence in the retail and consumer worlds, or brands that still maintain this status in some parts of the world but struggle in their homeland, such as Abercrombie & Fitch. Or, conversely, brands that can claim the status of

Lifestyle Brands in a regional area and are struggling to become a social phenomenon in an international market, such as Tod's.

We therefore wanted to represent four emblematic high-profile cases for their adherence to the model (Background, Manifesto and Expression are all recognisable and work seamlessly), and for their ability to last over time and become truly global social phenomenon. These two things are to be put into context: we can only define as 'Lifestyle' those brands that are led by a Visionary Leader, that are based on a strong Credo, that continuously feed their own mythology, and that can synthesise a suggested lifestyle through recognisable and iconic elements that are then transferred to products, communication and a retail experience. The cases that we selected, which of course are not exhaustive of the Lifestyle Brands universe, are Apple, Diesel, Patagonia, and Slow Food.

5.2 APPLE: A MANDATORY REFERENCE[1]

5.2.1 A couple of facts

In 2001, Apple Computer, a relatively small company with $5 billion in revenues, launched its first iPod in a world still in shock after September 11.

Ten years later, Apple reached $100 billion in revenues and 400 million iPods, the best-selling device in the history of mankind. From 2003 to 2008 Apple's stock value increased by 25 times, from $7.5 to $180 per share, until it reached $210 in 2010. Apple and Steve Jobs have received many awards, including *Advertising Age*'s 2003 Marketer of the Year and the *Fortune* CEO of the Decade. The company was considered by *Fortune* to be 'the most admired company' from 2008 to 2010.

In 2008, Brandchannel.com asked 2,000 readers from 170 countries which brand had the most impact on their lives: Apple won by far.

The success of the Apple Stores is striking: in 2011, the 300 Apple Stores in major cities around the world had been visited by an average of 15,000 customers per week and generated over $2 billion in profits and $9 billion in sales.

In 2011, the iTunes platform reached 200 million subscribed users around the world, selling more than 3 billion tracks of songs in a market that had been forecast to disappear. Apple has become the most valuable global brand, surpassing Google in the BrandZ Top 100 Most Valuable Global Brands 2011 ranking by Millward Brown, with an estimated value of over $153 billion. In August 2011, with about $337 billion of market capitalisation, Apple became the largest publicly traded company in the world, displacing the oil giant ExxonMobil, for years at the top of the rankings. The day Steve Jobs passed away, 6 October 2011, the company's market capitalisation was at $350 billion.

5.2.2 The reason Apple is a Lifestyle Brand

Starting out as a Cult Brand, Apple is now a reference point for hundreds of millions of consumers. Already in the period between 1989 and 1994, Apple customers became fans who worshipped Steve Jobs as an icon, celebrated Christmas at the MacWorld Expo in San Francisco, considered Cupertino a sort of Mecca and thought of Bill Gates as a kind of incarnation of evil. Those people still have an online community of reference: Cult of Mac.

The transition from Cult to Lifestyle took place starting in 2001, and was due to both an enlargement of the offer, with the launch of the iPod and subsequently the iPhone, as well as a consolidation of emotional and social brand associations. Consumer benefits go way beyond being purely rational, and even emotional. Like other Lifestyle Brands, Apple has been characterised by an explicit call to action: 'Think Different'. Still today, the global tribe of Apple customers feels part of a different group that wants to think differently, have the opportunity to express their opinion, and control and exploit the technology for their own pleasure and fulfilment. They love aesthetics and are comfortable with the language and power of images. Mac is not compatible? As argued by the Italian journalist Beppe Severgnini, 'with me it is, with Microsoft I don't care'.

5.2.3 Background (Credo and Stories)

Apple believes in the supremacy of individuals over technology, or, better, it believes in technologies that can free an individual. Apple believes in Uniqueness, in Difference, in Intelligence and Humour. Apple is Innovative, Elegant, Cool and Friendly. This can be considered its Credo.

Apple is also naturally full of Stories and is characterised by the creation and introduction of a series of iconic products. The company was born in 1976 in Steve Jobs' garage (owned by his parents); about ten years later the same manager who he had initially hired to run the company, Pepsi's former CEO John Sculley, fired Jobs. There are many legends regarding the famous 'bitten apple' logo. Initially the logo depicted Isaac Newton sitting under an apple tree, together with an inscribed quote saying, 'Newton, a mind forever voyaging through strange seas of thought'. It is said that the founders wanted a simple and immediate symbol and that co-founder Steve Wozniak wanted a name that starts with A to appear at the beginning of alphabetical orders and before Atari. Surely the bitten apple is an icon from the world of fairy tales, and it is simple, emphatic, non-conformist.

Introduced in 1984, the Macintosh offered an ease of use that was unheard of at its time: no external cables except for the power cable, a concept still followed today. The compact tower shape was unique in the category. The windows and icons built into the operating system made it very easy and intuitive to use. At its peak it was selling a product every 27 seconds. The famous TV commercial launching the Macintosh, with a girl who destroys a screen on which the film inspired by George Orwell's 1984 is being projected, aired only once during the Super Bowl. When Jobs returned to Apple in 1997, he assigned himself a salary of $1 per year as CEO.

As well as being Apple's relaunch product after the return of Steve Jobs, the 1998 iMac took on an 'all in one' concept with a unique design, becoming a pillar of Apple's offer.

In 2001 two products were launched: the iPod, defined by Steve Jobs as 'not a cheap MP3 player, but the best MP3 player', and the iMusic ecosystem, which in just a few years would revolutionise the music industry's distribution by digitalising it.

The Fifth Avenue store (the Cube) in New York, which opened in 2006, has become one of the most photographed landmarks in the world, open 24 hours a day, 365 days a year.

In 2007, Apple released its first iPhone: a touch screen and a button. In 2008, the MacBook Air became the thinnest notebook and laptop ever produced.

Steve Jobs never gave interviews. He was a tyrannical perfectionist ready to fire an employee on the spot, but also a charismatic leader who inspired creativity and dedication to the cause. His own battle with disease took on a mythic aura over time, up to the end.

5.2.4 Manifesto (Lifestyle Proposition and Codes)

'Changing the world – one person at a time' was Apple's slogan in the mid-1980s. And Apple has in fact changed the world it had found for the better. Since its first appearance, it has questioned man's relationship with technology thanks to an innovative user interface management and a search for a sensorial dialogue with the user himself.

As stated by Steve Jobs himself during MacWorld in San Francisco in 2005, Apple has become a lifestyle brand that owes much to his home in Cupertino, California:

> *At the centre of it all, Apple is now a lifestyle brand, rather than a technology company. Each iPod comes inscribed with the words 'designed in California', a seemingly throwaway statement that gives a fundamental insight into the company's outlook. The message is straightforward: we are innovators, we are cool, we are non-corporate, we are friendly. It's an extended new age mantra that betrays Apple's West Coast roots and has proved crucial to its image – both good and bad – over the years.[2]*

More precisely, Apple offers a way of life (Lifestyle Proposition) that, by making technology accessible, enhances people's individuality, their interpersonal skills, their imagination and their creativity. The iPod is a product that tells our story: it defines our identity through our music, pictures and videos. But at the same time, Apple also provides a sense of belonging to a cool and different community. The slogan 'Think Different' summed up in two words the Zen philosophy that Jobs had embraced since his conversion to Buddhism.

Apple products have always been unique and unmistakable. In terms of expression codes, however, stable elements tend to be relatively few: an undisputed trend towards minimalism, found mainly in the general 'cleanness' and generous space around the inevitable apple symbol on products, on packaging and in points of sale. There is the obsessive attention to detail; the use of aluminium for the PowerBook and white for accessories such as the power supply unit and the iPod headphones; the use of black as a colour counterpoint; and finally, the 'i' before the name of the product – iPods, iPad, iPhone, and more recently iCloud – is perhaps the element that best expresses Apple's take of a given day and age: the user as co-author of his own experience.

5.2.5 Expression (product, communication and experience)

Apple products and software are a whole world that provides the customer with a superior experience based on a design, a seductive choice of materials, an inimitable ease of use and an almost artisanal attention to stylistic and functional detail that would be suitable for a luxury product but is instead transferred to consumer products. The design of a functional product becomes pure sex appeal. Jobs was obsessed with tactile experiences coming from the opening of iPhone or iPad boxes. In addition Job's experience at Atari and with videogames made him understand the importance of keeping things simple. Apple's mantra has always been 'simplicity is the greatest sophistication, sleek but not slick'. The simplicity and intuitive ease of use facilitate individual contributions and the co-design of the experience itself.

The role of communication was key in Apple's history, even if the company can hardly be called a top spender in terms of media investment. Apple has always tried to use fairly high-impact campaigns that would stimulate discussion and word of mouth, without the fear of being provocative. Campaigns such as 'Think Different' or 'I am a Mac, I am a PC', which ironically compare Apple with Microsoft, represent landmarks in the history of communication. The main channel is still represented by MacWorld, the live product presentation events, whose newsworthiness does not escape news reporting from around the world. The difference between Jobs and other successful entrepreneurs lay precisely in his extraordinary ability to express himself during these events: the development of powerful 'storytelling' made up of personal stories, minimalist clothing and music to share.

The decision to open dedicated Apple stores in 2001 was born out of frustration of the disappointing experience offered by traditional retailers. The first store opening was in Virginia in 2001 and was preceded by adoring fans camping out the night before. From there, openings continued, and in most cases ended up representing hip destinations. A team of experts, including the former GAP CEO, carried out the store design, breaking the rules in the electronics industry.

The brand experience is expressed in spacious, bright and simple spaces, in task-oriented workdesks (video editing, digital photography, music management, etc.) available to browse and in the Genius Bar, an area where a team provides expert diagnostic and repair services. Often there are spaces in the store reserved for Apple Events, giving an opportunity for training or shows. Apple controls the customer experience by managing key variables such as staff training and the selection of the most prestigious locations, which feed traffic and image.

5.2.6 Visionary Leadership and organisational mechanisms

Steve Jobs has always claimed to be motivated not by money but by truly loving his work and his creation (Apple). He never worked to please the customer or to beat Microsoft but to make the best products on Earth. Ignited by the subculture of the American campus and the unique mix among Zen Buddhism and being vegetarian, drugs and contemplation, he found a way to transform the industries of music, entertainment and information technology, offering a unique and unmistakable perspective.

Apple's basic philosophy can be found in Jobs' now-famous commencement speech to Stanford University graduates in 2005. In this speech he recommended:

> *Your time is limited, so don't waste it living someone else's life. Don't be trapped by dogma – which is living with the results of other people's thinking. Don't let the noise of others' opinions drown out your own inner voice. And most important, have the courage to follow your heart and intuition. They somehow already know what you truly want to become. Stay hungry, stay foolish.*

In his ten years away from Apple (from 1985 to 1996), in which the company inevitably lost direction, Jobs bought (among other things) Pixar for $10 million from director George Lucas, making it the benchmark for the global computer graphics industry and becoming the largest animation studio in the world before selling it to Disney for $7.4 billion. Jobs' greatest capacity as a leader has been his analysis of a world in constant evolution, from whatever point of view he observed it. Jobs has been described as a genius, a magician, a designer and a businessman, a visionary but at the same time very focused on operational excellence, and as someone who has skilfully managed to combine individualism and team spirit. At the crossroads between art and technology accountability, Attention to Detail and Perfectionism are part of the company's commandments; Hiring the Best is another.

In fact no one, not even Steve Jobs, could have created a phenomenon like Apple by himself. He always looked forward, but knew how to surround himself with the best collaborators for technical solutions. From Steve Wozniak to Tim Cook, to whom he has passed the direction, Apple has been (especially today) in need of great managers who are able to transform the vision of its leader into a reality, day after day. The question remains of what Apple will become post-Steve Jobs and if there will be a new Visionary Leader capable of maintaining the same sensitivity towards its customers' tastes, have the ability to realise their wishes in advance and have a design talent that excites and improves lives.

5.3   DIESEL: BEYOND FASHION, A POINT OF VIEW ON THE WORLD[3]

5.3.1   A couple of facts

Diesel was the first non-American brand name to sell jeans to Americans. Since its establishment, Diesel has sold over 100 million jeans worldwide. In 1985, Renzo Rosso the visionary acquired ownership of company, and in 1988 hired Wilbert Das as creative director. Since the early 1990s, Diesel began to open stores around the world. Today, Diesel products are available in 5,000 stores, 300 of which are Directly Operated Stores. The Only The Brave group,[4] of which Diesel is the star, has a turnover over 1.3

billion Euros and has 6,000 employees located in 17 factories in Europe, Asia and America.

Notwithstanding the global scope of its company, Renzo Rosso has maintained a strong bond with its land, acquiring, for instance, over 100 hectares situated on the Marostica hills (Vicenza, Italy) to establish the Diesel Farm, which produces wine using antique techniques. In 2010, the new headquarters (Diesel Village) were inaugurated in the industrial area of Breganze, near Vicenza. This aimed at being a 'great place to work', thanks to the pleasing mix of residential and high-tech design. In 2011, Renzo Rosso published the book *Be Stupid For Successful Living*, apparently an ode to stupidity and nonsense, on which he further commented, saying, 'A lot of people considered me as stupid. But it's actually the stupid that see things the way they could be, not only the way they are.'[5]

5.3.2 The reason Diesel is a Lifestyle Brand

Diesel was born in the 1980s as a niche jeans brand characterised by different denim treatments and with a particularly 'worn out' feel. The name Diesel was chosen as an avant-garde symbol of the oil crisis of the 1970s and as an international word that could bring jeans brand worldwide success. In the words of Renzo Rosso: 'I did not think that Diesel would become a global brand overnight, but in the 1990s it was becoming a small cult in some countries around the world.'

In fact, next to the product, the Diesel brand immediately acquires emotional and social associations and getting adopted by the Gen X segment, young consumers born in the 1970s. This was a new type of customer for the fashion industry at that time: they were internationally homogenous, they watch the same movies, listened to the same music, went to the same places and wore the same things. This segment would eventually evolve over time, assuming other definitions but still remaining young, active and open to change. They possess a hypercritical attitude towards the media, but are still well-informed, reject pre-packaged ideologies but adopt without a problem brands that help express themselves. Diesel marketing strategy was able to attract this people by combining humour and political issues, two themes unprecedented in advertising before, through a distinctive tone of voice.

Diesel's transition from Cult to Lifestyle occurs by binding the brand to this category of people while expanding its presence in other segments towards a total look, which today includes leather goods, footwear, fragrances and home furnishings, up to Diesel 'spaces' – initiatives that are capable of transmitting the message and philosophy of the brand. Such as the project Diesel:U:Music launched in 2001: a worldwide collaborative music support network that has been tracking down unsung artists giving them a platform to the music industry.

5.3.3   Background (Credo and Stories)

According to Renzo Rosso,

> *Diesel has always, and will always, operate independently and instinctively – from the heart more than the head. Diesel is an attitude. It is about being brave, being confident with oneself, wanting to innovate and challenge, and never being satisfied. It means being open to new things and listening to your intuition. That's why emotion is one of our main drivers.*

Diesel offers an irreverent ideology, subversive but always playful, which expresses itself through values such as Provocation, Fantasy, Energy, Courage of Reinvention, Humour, Sensuality, Taste for Design and Entertainment.

Diesel is a company that does things in a very serious way, but doesn't take itself too seriously, and never forgets to have fun while searching for an original view of the world.

The Diesel story is a collection of significant moments in which it is possible to truly understand the brand's unconventional approach. In the 1990s, those who phoned the company were connected to the switchboard, which always answered with: 'Welcome to the Diesel Planet'.

In 1995, Diesel was the first fashion brand to appear on the Internet. Diesel opened its first store in 1996 in New York across the street from competitor Levi's on Lexington Avenue.

To collect the prize of 'Advertiser of the Year' at Cannes in 1998, four people jumped on stage with Renzo Rosso masks on. The invitation to the party to celebrate Diesel's thirty years was a video with cartoon inserts based on vintage 1970s porn movies. There are many other examples, and last but not least mention should be made to the Only The Brave Foundation, a not-for-profit organisation created by Rosso to mobilise and empower youth to 'be brave' and end extreme poverty by donating not only money but also their voices and ideas.

5.3.4 Manifesto (Lifestyle Proposition and Codes)

'Being able to be daring, go to the limit, and not be afraid to see and do things differently from others' is the spirit of the founder Renzo Rosso, which is summarised in the concept 'Only the Brave': only those with courage and who dare will win. It is a philosophy that we find in the first Diesel claim, then in a perfume and today even in the name of the holding company that controls the Diesel brand. True to its motto since the beginning, Diesel has contributed to changing the clothing industry in terms of production, communication and distribution. It remained faithful to the intent of being the most original, bold, irreverent, funny, sexy, conscious, practical, innovative and relevant Lifestyle Brand.

On this basis, Diesel started a dialogue with its customers by offering 'Guides to Successful Living for People Interested in General Health and Mental Power', a particularly ironic, disenchanted and cool way to see the world. 'We wanted to do something that appealed to us, of which we would be the first customers' said Renzo Rosso. It is an ideology that can be summed up in the call to action 'For Successful Living' before and 'Be Stupid' subsequently, expressing a degree of continuity and a further dose of provocation. Contradiction is part of the brand DNA: a vintage look with contemporary soul, a name that draws on a heavy industry for a fashion brand, the obsession with quality and deliberate search for defects in the product.

Diesel has a variety of characteristic codes, starting with the diagonally placed label with the logo. The brand's Expression stems from the industrial and vintage worlds, and from here also the 'stone washed' and 'dirty denim' jeans treatments, which are certainly a Diesel code. Over time, its rugged soul, work wear, denim, vintage or urban modern cowboy/cowgirl evolved into new stylistic codes in terms of processed materials, matched in unexpected ways such as treated leather paired with denim, and small metal decorations.

These contradictory codes have also been transferred to perfume: 'Fuel for Life' for women reminds us of an alcohol flask but wrapped in lace.

5.3.5 Expression (product, communication and experience)

Jeans, intended as workwear, are part of the corporate DNA. They are worn for comfort but also because they make you feel free. The company goal, however, has always been to experiment with innovative technologies, leaving a worn look to the product. Rosso himself has often spoken of customers in Italy who sent back products thinking they were faulty. In the States, however, there was a greater culture for this type of product, and that is where the brand's success was born. The Diesel jean has a soul, it's rock, strong, tough, and it's a product that has a life to itself. 'I grew up in the era of rock and roll, listening to artists like Black Sabbath and the Sex Pistols. Much of this rock and roll attitude has played a large role in what Diesel has become' says Rosso.

Diesel's approach to communication has always been to provide opportunities for entertainment and food for thought around a certain way of seeing the world. As once again, Renzo Rosso says: 'We do not advertise but communicate, we consider this our "face". The product is communication and communication is the product. It is a whole system, a way of life, it's the "Successful Living" which we create together with the client.'[6]

Diesel campaigns as we know them began in 1991, and since then have always been characterised by a single creative concept worldwide. This concept is developed within the company by the Diesel Creative Team, in partnership with external agencies, a process that allows the company to maintain the integrity of their identity over time.

The slogan 'For Successful Living', interpreted with different themes in different seasons, was born as a parody of traditional post-World War II advertising that promised a better life to those who bought a certain brand or a product, a promise that can only be seen as ironic for Diesel's disenchanted public. In fact, the promise of 'success' that is found in many Diesel campaigns is exaggerated and deliberately made absurd.

Initially the choice of media was very consistent with the unconventional message, favouring publications like *Wired*, *Out* (a gay magazine) or MTV, given that Diesel was an early supporter of theirs. The new 2010 campaign 'Be Stupid: to be Stupid is to be Brave' was initially very controversial: of course, Lifestyle Brands are by definition discriminatory, and the call to action in this case was particularly provocative. Later it was better appreciated because it interprets the spirit of current mass culture as well as the Diesel brand values, as all the campaigns that preceded it had done.

The Diesel store experience can be summed up with one term: 'eclectic'. Even within an environment that maintains the codes of the brand, that is, the warehouse, the industrial workspace and vintage, each store interprets these codes according to specific points of view in order to offer an unmistakable, up-to-date Diesel experience in each place. The items are presented in a 'theatrical' but ironic way, behind curtains and frames that are entertaining to the customer. Following the coexistence of opposites logic, heterogeneous materials coexist in store such as steel and wood, dimly lit areas that remind us of a warehouse space contrast with brightly coloured areas like the children's corner. Wi-Fi locations connect the customer to the virtual Diesel store with the ability to view other products, while a web camera allows customers to take photos wearing Diesel garments, upload to Facebook and share with their network. The events organised by the company for the launch of new seasons would deserve a whole separate chapter. These are memorable evenings during which customers can clearly see the Diesel life-style come to life.

5.3.6 Visionary Leadership and organisational mechanisms

Renzo Rosso, founder and owner of Diesel, was born in 1955 and, just as for many Visionary Leaders, his personal and professional life merged in an inseparable way: 'Diesel is not my company, it's my life.' Following its leader, the Diesel brand never claimed irreverence or tried to be cool. It has always been cool and irreverent by doing what no other company dared.

Rosso is a man who designs the future, looks ahead, tries to work out what his fans will want through time, doesn't look at daily sales (a task given to a structured manage-ment team) but instead cultivates his creative vision. He is a young spirit, obsessed about creativity, change and new technologies.

The founder managed to evolve over time thanks to the team of people he surrounded himself with, and agrees: 'The strength of Diesel lies in its team'; 'There isn't a "crea-tive genius" behind the products, but a close-knit vision-ary group we call Diesel Creative Team.' When asked 'how can one continue to surprise?' Rosso replies that the prod-uct and the design department must always remain at the centre of the vision. Diesel scouts talent every year about a thousand design schools to insert young people in the company, whose energy revitalises the energy of the com-pany itself. This is how Rosso maintains the connection open between the Visionary Leader and the rest of the organisation.

5.4 PATAGONIA: ECO-SUSTAINABILITY AS A LIFESTYLE[7]

5.4.1 A couple of facts

Yvon Chouinard, who initially sold climbing equipment, launched Patagonia in 1974, as a brand with 'romantic visions of glaciers tumbling into fjords, jagged windswept peaks, gauchos and condors'.[8]

In 1977, Patagonia introduced the Pile Fleece Jacket; nowadays any outdoor apparel brand offers at least one version of this product.

Following a 1993 research study, where Chouinard unexpectedly found out that industrial cotton fibre had the highest environmental impact, Patagonia decided to convert all its production to organic cotton in less than two years, making the use of this material a new standard for the industry.

It became an obsession as well as a courageous choice, which initially put at risk the profitability of the company but it paid off in the long term. In this regard Chouinard used to say: 'Every time we do the right thing for the environment, we make a profit.'

In 2008, the company won the Eco Brand of the Year in the Volvo Sports Design Awards; in 2009, it received the Corporate Leadership Award from AIGA and it won two Gear of the Year Awards in 2010.

Patagonia has been named by *Fortune* as one of the 100 Best Companies to Work for in the world and is listed among the top 25 medium-sized companies by the Great Place to Work Institute.

The Cleanest Line blog, accessible by employees, customers and fans, discusses issues of product functionality and performance but mostly advertises matters of environmental concern. The Cleanest Line is at the top of Compete rank, ninth in Alexa rank and fourteenth in the ranking of corporate blog Blogrank, according to which it is also the first in terms of number of visitors per month. Since 1973 over $10 million have been donated thanks to a self-imposed Earth tax. Each year the company has contributed 10 per cent of annual profits (or 1 per cent of sales, whichever is greater) to hundreds of environmental groups. The company has been one of the few to prosper despite the economic crisis of recent years. Currently it has 1,500 employees and earned revenues of $340 million in 2010, increasing to $410 million in 2011.

5.4.2 The reason Patagonia is a Lifestyle Brand

> *Function always dictates the form – and the perfect form is the result of a perfectly solved functional need.*

Following this motto by the founder, Patagonia became an authority in the 1980s in technical fabrics for outdoor use. The strong relationship with the community of users/customers rapidly transformed Patagonia into a cult brand. Subsequently, the unconventional use of colour and communication, and the expansion in product range from climbing to skiing, fishing and surfing, have gradually extended the space occupied by the brand. All the sports that Patagonia has entered are 'silent' sports, lacking an audience, engines and environmental impact. This favours a spiritual union between man and nature. Furthermore, as it attracted an increasingly large segment of people, the brand grew in social and emotional associations. Patagonia is certainly known for quality products and a strong specialisation in outdoor, but it is mainly characterised by a clear and distinctive philosophy that has inspired an extraordinary commitment on environmental issues from employees and customers over time.

Customers are defined as Patagoniacs: they are evange-
lists of nature as well as of the brand itself. Patagonia has a
number of 'ambassadors'. These are not only athletes but
also people who have experienced the products and have
become spokesmen/women through their extraordinary
experiences. Since 1990, the Field Reports, which are testi-
monies by athletes, travellers and adventurers collected on
the frontiers of nature, have contributed to the dialogue
between the brand and its followers, and fuel its legend.

5.4.3   Background (Credo and Stories)

To climb mountains you need to trust others. The origins of
the climbing world set the foundations for a brand based on
sharing and teamwork. The concept of trust within and outside the company, in connection with the ambassadors and
customers, is a central point in explaining Patagonia's success.
Its Credo can be summed up with the values of Simplicity,
Freedom, Integrity and Love for Nature, and can be inferred
from slogans like 'No bound by convention' or 'The more you
know, the less you need' and from its tag line, which again
is a call to action addressed to all the followers: 'Committed
to the Core.' Patagonia is rich in Stories that have built and
continue to nourish the legend, from the name, which orig-
inates from an epic journey made by the founder in 1968
from California to the borders of Argentina. It is a name that
is already full of suggestions and meanings, as well as known
and pronounceable in all languages of the world.

Similarly, the logo is the skyline of Cerro Fitzroy looking
west, in Patagonia. True to the original vision, Patagonia
embraced the green movement decades before it became
a social necessity and mass phenomenon. The company's
origin also comes from an intuition of the founder, who
wanted to replace the traditional steel spikes used for climbing with aluminium cabletray, which causes less damage

to the rock and can easily be removed while leaving no trace. Hence the idea of 'clean climbing', which continued in the direction of using environmentally friendly materials, promoting eco-friendly products, using only organic cotton or being the first brand to create product lines made from recycled plastic, patented as CRP.

The clothing business started after Chouinard was spotted climbing wearing colourful rugby jerseys he had imported from England. From then on, colour would become a distinctive feature of a Patagonia product.

On the brand's website, you can find out how many miles the raw materials travelled before being used, how much energy was needed to produce a garment, and the 'costs' in terms of carbon dioxide emissions. A revolutionary internship programme supports employees to work up for up to two months in a non-profit environmental group of their choice.

5.4.4 Manifesto (Lifestyle Proposition and Codes)

The curved and tiny style of the Patagonia logo is reminiscent of old travel map prints and suggests a feeling of romanticism in contrast to the technical nature of the garments. This sense of romanticism can also be found in Patagonia's promised lifestyle (Lifestyle Proposition), which can be summarised in a 'genuine outdoor spirit leaving only footprints'.

Those who wear Patagonia look for quality, durability and innovation, but want to be part of a group of individuals who feel active and confident, and are characterised by high social responsibility towards the environment and others. These are people who prefer a morning surf in the ocean or an epic climb rather than a day spent in theme parks or experiencing pre-packaged tourist villages.

They are a rough and adventurous group of people who chase outdoor life and entertainment and who embody the dirt bag culture: living in the moment and collecting photographs without leaving traces of their passage. Patagonia is deliberately neither affordable nor trendy. Regarding the characteristic lifestyle codes, the microfleece is certainly a trait that represents the brand. In addition, colours are used in an unconventional manner: Cobalt, Aloe, Seafoam and Iced Mocha are classics that have redefined the look of the people who experience nature intensively. The interiors of the shops are made of high-quality FSC-certified wood.

5.4.5 Expression (product, communication and experience)

The Patagonia product experience is based on its functionality. Patagonia ambassadors work closely with the Design Department to test, develop and validate the products in the most challenging corners of the planet. The authority in technical textiles is still today reflected in the names that distinguish the different materials, some more than twenty years old. Synchilla Fleece was the first alternative to natural fibres, H2No® Waterproof Barrier is a completely waterproof and windproof fabric, Capilene Performance Baselayers fabrics are completely recyclable and able to control odours. Product communication is characterised by transparency and honesty: the promise isn't about products that do not pollute (as Jen Rapp, the Director of Communications and Public Relations says, pollution occurs just by performing an economic activity), but about products that pollute as little as possible, consistent with available technology.

The relatively low visibility of the brand before 2000 reflected the fact that the company believed its environmental actions would speak louder than words. However, consumer research in those years showed that the actual difference in commitment towards the environment compared to competitors was not well perceived. The company decided to step up its efforts, focusing on a fewer relevant environmental issues. Since then, Patagonia has continued to deliver strong ideological messages, policy proposals and actions towards environmental protection, fuelling the mythology and an exchange of outdoor life experiences through highly interactive communication and unconventional instruments. Customers are regularly involved with campaigns such as 'Capturing a Patagoniac', in which the stores encourage people to send pictures of their adventures. Another initiative, the 'Dirt Bag Grant', is an award that celebrates the idea of doing more with less. The 'Footprint Chronicles' help fans understand the path taken by a leader of an expedition. The brand ambassadors share experiences from the field in The Cleanest Line Blog, as well as in The Tin Shed video channel, or on YouTube.

Patagonia's communication executions portray nature's beauty as well as its challenges. People often feel small and alone within the immensity of space, and the company's publicity describes man's insignificance in comparison with nature.

Patagonia does not have a large number of directly operated stores, but this is the result of the company's vision of maintaining an easy-to-control size. In setting up its own stores, Patagonia selects historic sites and buildings. In developing its retail concept, it tries to preserve the integrity of the building itself. For example, in Covent Garden, London, the shop occupies the space of the old Watney Combe & Reid brewery, founded in 1837.

5.4.6 Visionary Leadership and organisational mechanisms

Patagonia is one of the few brands that has managed to maintain its integrity and authenticity over time. It has not felt the need to dilute its brand essence to grow in unrelated segments, and has remained focused instead on its core businesses. This has been able to happen mainly because the company is still in the hands of the founder, Yvon Chouinard, the very personification of a Visionary Leader. Chouinard is a living legend within the climbing community for having redesigned all the equipment and clothing for the discipline with continuous innovation. But he also has a very creative vision for his company: Chouinard says that in climbing, reaching the top of the mountain doesn't matter, what counts is how you reach it. Similarly, in business he suggests not to look at the profits, but at the way the company can solve a need: the profit will follow.

Chouinard is neither the company president nor the CEO. He is known as the Company Philosopher, the one who redefines the direction for new opportunities, as happened during the transition from technical mountain gear to the surf and swim world, and to environmental causes.

In Chouinard's own words in an interview with *Fortune*: 'We're getting into the surf market, because it's never going to snow again, and the waves are going to get bigger and bigger.'[9] The problem with many companies is that their leaders are focused on the day-to-day realities, leaving behind the original vision and not always capturing changes in the market or in the world.

Thanks to his powerful ideology, Chouinard has always been able to keep the company's cultural values alive, even in difficult years such as in 1991 when he was forced to lay off 120 employees (almost a fifth of the workforce) for the first time ever. It was then that, together with his managers, he decided to go on a five-day trip to share the mission and principles that should guide the company. From that trip he drew inspiration for his book *Let My People Go Surfing*: a philosophy, a vision of the world and a powerful internal and external source of inspiration. The central concept is that people must be independent and must know how to motivate themselves: it doesn't matter when people work, what matters are the results they reach. It was an element of innovation in Patagonia's organisational culture that led to breaking boundaries between work and leisure, family and colleagues. Children can be brought to the office and staff can engage in sports at any time of the day.

What is defined as 'personnel' in business textbooks, in Patagonia is known as an extended family, which as a whole is the mechanism that allows the transfer of the leader's vision to everyday operations. The president and CEO of Patagonia, David Olsen, once said that 'Patagonia cannot build great quality products without a great quality work environment.'[10] A shared leadership, based on authentic values is certainly the secret of success for this long-lasting brand.

5.5 SLOW FOOD: CHANGE THE WORLD, ONE BITE AT A TIME[11]

5.5.1 A couple of facts

Originally set up in 1986 by a group of culturally engaged youngsters as the 'Arcigola' gastronomic association in the Langhe area of Piedmont (Italy), the International Slow Food Movement was actually founded in Paris three years later. Since then there have been many initiatives to defend local food traditions and foster people's interest in what they eat and how this affects the condition of our planet. Their aim is to fight the standardisation of taste and culture, and the power of agro-food industry multinationals.

Today Slow Food is a global, non-profit, grassroots organisation with supporters in 150 countries and over 100,000 members grouped in 1,300 Convivia (Slow Food local chapters), and a network of 2,000 food communities who produce quality foods sustainably and on a small scale.

Slow Food pursues its mission through a range of activities, including an extensive family of printed publications, the world's largest high-quality food fair (The 'Salone del Gusto'), a programme of international conferences, special projects such as Presidium[12] and Ark of Taste,[13] and the opening in 2004 of the University of Gastronomic Sciences in Pollenzo (Cuneo, Italy). In 2004, the Food & Agriculture Organization officially recognised Slow Food as a non-profit organisation. Its founder, Carlo Petrini, has been named 'European Hero' by *Time* magazine and 'one of the 50 people who could save the planet' by the *Guardian*. In 2012, Petrini was invited to speak on the right to food and food sovereignty at the 11th session of the United Nations Permanent Forum on Indigenous Issues, the first time an external guest had been asked to address the Forum.

More recently, the 'Slow Movement' has developed into a subculture in other areas with organisations including Slow Cities, Slow Living, Slow Travel and Slow Design.

5.5.2 The reason why Slow Food is a Lifestyle Brand

Slow Food began life as a popular movement and has evolved into a collective Lifestyle Brand. Basically representing a community of people looking for an alternative to the unauthentic and unhealthy lifestyles characterised by fast food and a fast life, Slow Food embeds a social benefit in its brand. While it started out as a cult for an elite of discerning and sometimes visionary consumers who were willing to combine the pleasure of good food with a genuine commitment to their community and the environment, today the Slow Food name and logo are present in many different segments, including publishing, education and events, positioned at the crossroads of ecology, gastronomy, ethics and pleasure.

Slow Food has a strong point of view that inspires a pattern of relationship, consumption and behaviour: the original intuition of the movement was summarised in a 'Manifesto', which today continues to be the format used to encapsulate the *raison d'être* and aspiration of new initiatives, such as the University of Gastronomic Sciences or the 'Ark of Taste'.

Slow Food has a Visionary Leader, Carlo Petrini, who has been its prophet and guiding light for the last twenty years, creating a network-based organisational mechanism that allows Slow Food to pursue its mission all over the world. Originally based on trust and a shared vision, the organisation became more and more structured in terms of roles and mechanisms, while maintaining a sense of mission among the 150 people who work at Slow Food headquarters in Bra. Slow Food raises funds by acting as an adviser and through commissions, donations and sponsorships, which it reinvests in innovative cultural projects.

5.5.3 Background (Credo and Stories)

Slow Food has a very rich Credo that is expressed by its very name: 'slow', meaning 'a way to regain wisdom and liberate the world from the "velocity" that is driving it forward on the road to extinction'.[14] In more detail, the approach adopted by Slow Food to agriculture, food production and gastronomy is based on a concept of food quality defined by three interconnected tenets: Good (a fresh and flavoursome seasonal diet that satisfies the senses and is part of our local culture), Clean (food production and consumption that do not harm the environment, animal welfare or our health), and Fair (accessible prices for consumers and fair conditions and pay for small-scale producers). The more emotional side of the brand is built on the benefits of Pleasure, Hedonism, Enjoyment, Tranquillity and Conviviality.

Slow Food Stories recount the food and drink experiences of Carlo Petrini and his friends as they wandered from one 'Osteria' to the next in Piedmont at the beginning of this adventure.[15] But the destiny of Carlo Petrini had probably already been written when he was born, because his nurse's name was 'Gola' ('Throat', a very unusual first name in Italian). In his infancy, the founder of Slow Food spent a great deal of time at his grandmother's house and built up a priceless body of knowledge about the customs and flavours of a rural society that was dying out. As Petrini himself says: 'My grandmother made jam and preserves for the winter, plucked chickens and skinned rabbits, and then cooked them with patience and a horror of wasting anything. In the right seasons she went out into the fields to gather wild herbs and salad.'[16]

Later, as a sociology student and activist, Petrini acquired a remarkable sensitivity towards politics, civil rights and communication. In fact, among other things, he was the founder of Radio Bra Onde Rosse, the first free broadcaster in Europe, which received support from numerous intellectuals, including future Nobel Literature Prize winner Dario Fo, because free broadcasts were still illegal at the time.

Two important events in 1986 probably convinced Petrini that Italy needed a better approach to food: the first was the opening of the first Italian branch of McDonald's next to the Spanish Steps in the very heart of Rome; the second was the death of 19 consumers and the poisoning of hundreds of others by cheap wine cut with methanol.

5.5.4 Manifesto (Lifestyle Proposition and Codes)

As reported by *USA Today*, Slow Food is everything that fast food is not. It is slow both to make and to eat. It is fresh, not processed. It is from neighbourhood farms and stores, not industrial growers. The 'Manifesto' issued in 1986 clearly outlined a Lifestyle Proposition:

> *Let us defend ourselves against the universal madness of 'the fast life' with tranquil material pleasures [...] we propose the vaccine of an adequate portion of sensual gourmandise pleasures, to be taken with slow and prolonged enjoyment [...] by cultivating taste, rather than impoverishing it, by stimulating progress, by encouraging international exchange programs, by endorsing worthwhile projects, by advocating historical food culture and by defending old-fashioned food traditions.*[17]

Slow Food believes that we all have a fundamental right to the pleasure of good food, and must therefore bear the responsibility of protecting the heritage of expertise, tradition and culture that makes this pleasure possible. As food is tied to many aspects of life, including culture, politics, agriculture and the environment, Slow Food is now an active player in a wide variety of areas, from education to agricultural policy. And its philosophy is perfectly encapsulated in a call to action: 'Faced with the excesses of modernization, we should no longer seek to change the world, but to save it.'

The Ark (a biblical metaphor) and Presidia programmes turned Slow Food members into heroes fighting to save our cultural roots and ecosystems.

While the Lifestyle Proposition is richly varied, the brand's typical expressive codes are limited to the snail icon and a characteristic naming of the main initiatives, using highly evocative names that draw their inspiration from Latin, like 'Convivia', 'Presidia' or 'Terra Madre'.

The snail logo, which originally appeared in a 1607 book about food, demonstrates the growing importance of historical as well as geographical roots, and is clearly an icon of slowness.

Some visual codes typical of the brand's origins and close relationship with the left-wing press have been lost over the years and tend to remain only in a few brand expressions, such as the graphical layout used by the organisation's guidebooks, for example.

5.5.5 Expression (product, communication and experience)

While its status as a brand is not defined by shops, food products or traditional communication campaigns, Slow Food is a brand in the most modern sense of the term. It has its own culture, world view and precise narrative formats: the icon of the snail acts from time to time as an umbrella or endorsement brand, adapting as needed to specific contexts.

The 'products' offered by Slow Food are basically publications. Since 1989, numerous guides, recipe books, essays, itineraries, studies, research projects, manuals and magazines have contributed to describing the movement's philosophy (in praise of pleasure, the development of taste and the protection of biodiversity), to enhancing the value of high-quality food and wine production, to protecting artisan specialties, plant varieties and animal species at risk of extinction and, finally, to promoting clean agriculture and high-quality gastronomy. Its supporters live the Slow Food experience through multiple events that bring together institutional stakeholders, producers and consumers. The most important is Terra Madre, the top meeting for food communities worldwide. The first convention was held in 2004 in Italy and was attended by 5,000 producers from 130 countries. The second edition in 2006 grew to include participation by 1,000 cooks, aware of the importance of their role in supporting local, high-quality production, as well as 400 researchers and academics seeking to build a bridge between their theoretical work and hands-on knowledge. In 2008, 1,000 young producers, cooks, students and activists from around the world also joined the network.

But of course there are also more hedonistic opportunities: Slow Food organises some of the world's major food events – Salone del Gusto, Cheese, Slow Fish – as well as many smaller fairs, to showcase sustainable agriculture and artisan food production, and connect producers with consumers who want to be aware of the impact of their food choices.

Finally, Slow Food played a key role in the creation and success of Eataly, which in just three years has established itself in Italy and worldwide as a winning retail format and an incomparable benchmark for fine food and wine. For Eataly, Slow Food acts as a strategic consultant, with the task of controlling and checking that the quality of the product proposed is always in line with the promise and that the producers presented by Eataly do not compromise on the quality of their products to satisfy growing demand.

5.5.6 Visionary Leadership and organisational mechanisms

Carlo Petrini's legendary charisma, passion and conviction are reflected in the popularity of the movement. Petrini is a visionary who works to improve the world's agriculture and food supply, one bite at a time. Starting from the idea that food satisfies both physical and social needs in humans, Petrini has succeeded in an extremely valuable intellectual operation: to restore dignity to the science of gastronomy in a world dominated by consumption and profit, managing to refocus attention on the central role played by food in our lives. It is an important story, because it reminds us that even the most important cultural adventures can spring from an enjoyable and hedonistic approach to life, far from the dusty cathedrals of knowledge, as was the case for Steve Jobs, Renzo Rosso or Yvon Chouinard. Great people are even greater if they know how to be serious when faced with that which is facetious and have a light touch when faced with serious issues: Petrini, notwithstanding his contradictions, embodies this very form of greatness. He is a unique, overflowing personality with remarkable oratorical powers, who has made converts throughout the world and built a global movement even though he only speaks Italian with a strong Piedmont accent. His book published in 2005, *Slow Food Revolution*, describes the pillars of the slow culture that has influenced the attitudes, opinions and interests of its followers and therefore their lifestyles.

The path that has delineated the philosophy of the Slow Food movement over the years has always been characterised by Petrini's remarkable propensity to embark on concrete initiatives that in some way put his thoughts into practice: the multiple associations of Slow Food, the ability to build major international events and the creation of the University of Gastronomic Sciences are only a few examples of his pragmatic verve and ability to engage human energy and resources around projects that seemed visionary, at first sight.

The network of 100,000 Slow Food associates is divided into local offices (known as Condotte in Italy and Convivium worldwide), coordinated by Convivium leaders who organise courses, tastings, dinners and trips, promote campaigns launched by the association at local level, activate broad-based projects such as school market gardens, and take part in major international events organised by Slow Food.

In an interview with the daily newspaper *Il Sole 24 Ore* in June 2009,[18] Carlo Petrini said that he intended to leave the movement he had founded because he had 'come to the end of the line'. He said that the movement was strong and had deep roots, and that where he himself hasn't been able to go, his successors would. At present more than 1,000 Slow Food Conviviums are active in 130 countries, including 410 Condotte in Italy: the organisation mechanisms to perpetuate the slow philosophy and its impact on our lives have been set in motion.

5.6 ARE YOU NOT A LIFESTYLE BRAND? PERHAPS THIS IS WHY

Lifestyle Brands are characterised by all the key components of the model and present a harmonious balance between them. An imbalance among these components or the lack or weakness of some of them, may therefore explain the difference between a successful Lifestyle Brand and an unfinished, unfocused or declining one. For each component, we can identify a specific function, a critical success factor and a way to measure its effectiveness, as in Table 5.1.

It is also possible to make an initial diagnosis of a Lifestyle Brand by considering some basic steps that we have covered in this book.

- Do you know what you believe in?
  The absence or inability to identify and express the profound values upon which the brand was built on makes

TABLE 5.1   The construction of Lifestyle Brands

	Component	Definition	Function	Critical success factor	Measurement of effectiveness
BACKGROUND	CREDO	Values that express the unique and original point of view of a brand	AGGREGATION	SOCIAL RELEVANCE	IMPACT ON CORPORATE CULTURE
	STORIES	Stories and anecdotes that have the power to engage the audience and fuel the mythology of the brand	INTEREST	MEMORABILITY	REPUTATION AND BRAND IMAGE
MANIFESTO	LIFESTYLE PROPOSITION	A proposed way of life that the audience can identify with	IDENTIFICATION	RELATIVE (OR POLARISING) RELEVANCE	IMPACT ON COMPANY ATTITUDES, VIEWS AND INTERESTS
	LIFESTYLE CODES	Specific codes that make the Manifesto immediately recognisable	RECOGNISABILITY	DIFFERENTIATION	ICONIC FEATURES
EXPRESSION	COMMUNICATION INTERACTION PRODUCT	How the Brand Manifesto becomes tangible through products, communication and direct interaction with the customer	STAGE SETTING	COHERENCE WITH THE MANIFESTO	ADOPTION

it almost impossible to meet social and emotional needs. The values, however, need to be strong: they need to polarise and inspire a group of followers.

- Do you have stories that deserve to be told?
  The absence or lack of relevant, interesting and memorable stories related to the brand (Stories), or of anecdotes that you would want to tell your friends, prevents the generation of word of mouth, which is a fundamental mechanism for propagation of information between people who feel part of the same group. Stories must be a wise blend of heritage and innovation. The prevalence of heritage risks keeping the brand anchored to the past, and not feeding enough reasons to renew interest, repurchase or extend into other categories. On the other hand, a sequence of novelties and unmemorable news, with no real roots or a strong emotional impact, does not help build a narrative, or a story with its own continuity. In the best-case scenario, they will describe a temporary trend.

- Is your Lifestyle Proposition still relevant?
  The world turns, people age, cultural references change. Sometimes the brand is anchored in the original intuition of its visionary leader while the world and consumers go elsewhere. Are you sure that your vision of the world, the brand's point of view on things, is still relevant?

- Are all elements well connected to each other?
  If the Lifestyle Proposition does not reflect in a logical and immediate manner both the Background and the Visionary Leader's thoughts, what the customer perceives is likely to be different from what the brand wants to really be (or is).

- Do you show yourself for who you really are?
  The Expression must unequivocally and without hesitation reveal the spirit of the Lifestyle Proposition.

If what the customer perceives through the product, communication and experience does not fully represent the Lifestyle Proposition, the brand isn't fully using all of its potential.

- Is the organisation able to transform its vision into reality?

  If it is the people who really make up a company, it is even truer that it is the people who make up Lifestyle Brands. Typically, in the latter, the Visionary Leader surrounds himself with capable people who are also able to transfer the vision to products, retail, and coherent and successful communications campaigns on a day-by-day basis. These are people who share the vision, who are proud to work in the company, and are testimonials of their own Brand Manifesto. When the organisational mechanisms are poorly structured, or do not fully express the vision of the leader, it is very difficult to ensure the stability and ability to evolve the brand consistently over time and space through other categories. Often in this situation, the brand is forced to regain credibility and success season after season and cannot achieve or maintain a stable Lifestyle Brand status over time.

- Do you continue to nourish your initial vision?

  Finally, if the brand loses its original promise, it loses its foundations, its basis for uniqueness and differentiation. This is true for all brands. The success of Lifestyle Brands over time depends on the ability to remain true to the original spirit and keep up the interest of the core followers ensuring the integrity of the brand. Re-editing iconic products by adding new attributes or features and celebrating past stories with exhibitions and events is not enough. It is necessary to maintain authority in the original product category that initially gave birth to the brand: if this authority is lost, the brand loses focus and can move to the Solution Brands area. To keep this authority, the brand must continue to invest and innovate in its historic product lines to keep their leadership, and continue to engage in dialogue with the customers concerning those products to capture every nuance in the evolution of their culture and their needs.

APPENDIX

THE ECONOMIC IMPACT AND FINANCIAL EQUITY OF THE BRAND

There is a general awareness about the importance and the role of brands in determining the economic performance of a company. As we saw in Chapter 2, the value (or equity) of a brand comes from its ability to enhance a product or service by creating a relationship and a lasting emotional connection with consumers. This phenomenon leads the product or service away from the land of poorly differentiated commodities and lays the foundation for increasing current clients' loyalty, generating interest in new ones, and applying a premium price in a sustainable manner over time.

All this surely affects sales, but the value of the brand is also reflected into the bottom line: for example, the attractiveness of the company in respect to human resources can help to keep labour costs under control: people know that an experience for a top brand is more appreciated and sellable in the labour market and are therefore willing to accept a lower compensation.

In other words, strong brands have the power to increase profitability and growth, reducing risks and costs. According to some authors, including Scott Davis,[1] strong brands are considered more important by their consumers, and for this reason they:

- generate the possibility of applying a premium price;
- fuel customer loyalty, increasing profitability per capita;
- are taken into consideration for purchase, reducing the costs of acquiring new customers;
- create opportunities to extend towards other targets, categories and countries;
- start from a well-established reputation, making it less expensive to launch new products (compared to less diverse competitors);
- generate greater returns on investment in marketing and communications;
- are 'forgiven' or are given the benefit of the doubt when things go less well or products are less successful;
- always give the opportunity to reconsider them to those who hadn't initially done so;
- have greater negotiating power with their distribution and trading partners.

Furthermore:

- they allow the management of extraordinary transactions such as mergers, acquisitions, IPOs, etc. from a greater bargaining power position;
- they allow access to new financial resources, optimising the company's financial management. It is indeed possible to use the brand in medium-term financing operations (IP-Loan), or by securitising royalties rising from licensing activities (IP Securitisation), or realising combined sales operations and a simultaneous lease of the transaction asset (IP Sale-Lease Back).[2]

But it is also possible to quantify more precisely the specific contribution of the brand to the company's financial performance starting from market research objective data.

A study of BrandAsset Consulting based on Young & Rubicam's Brand Asset™ Valuator data (see Chapter 2), showed that brands that reach the Leadership status, recording the highest levels of Differentiation, Relevance, Esteem and Familiarity, have a higher probability of achieving growth rates in sales and higher EBITDA margins.[3] Another conclusion by the same study is that the impact of the brand varies considerably across categories, being significantly higher for symbol intensive brands.

Millward Brown Optimor's BrandZ™ (see Chapter 2) analysed the Top 100 Most Valuable Global Brands as a 'stock portfolio' over seven years (2006 to 2012), finding a highly favourable performance compared to a current stock market index, the S&P500 (see Figure A1). While in that period the S&P was down more than it was up and appreciated

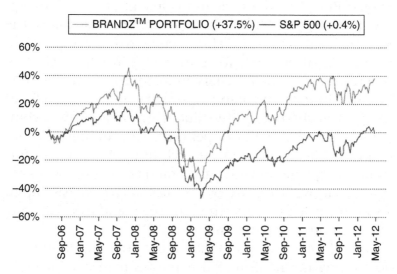

Figure A1 **BrandZ™ portfolio vs S&P 500**
Source: *Bloomberg*, Millward Brown Optimor, BrandZ™ Data.

only 4.5 per cent, in contrast the BrandZ™ portfolio increased by 46.3 per cent. Like the S&P 500, the BrandZ™ portfolio comprises a diverse group of public companies, including the strongest brands in the BrandZ™ ranking. The comparison between the two portfolios shows that strong brands outperform the stock market benchmark by a wide margin.

The conclusion is that changes in the perception of consumers and the health of the brand clearly influence the changes in market value and total value of a company. In addiction, considering the fluctuating economic climate of the period, we can say that strong brands have performed better both in times of economic expansion and contraction.

It is guessed that the high differentiation, low substitutability, visibility and prestige of these brands typically emphasise the economic impact of the brand itself: in fact, when an individual must meet a basic need (such as cleaning the house) and the potential product substitutability is high, price and accessibility become key factors in the choice. But when the same individual has the need to represent him or herself, he/she is much more tolerant of the price, and increases the effort required to get the brand or the sought product. To confirm this insight, according to a research on the jewellery industry conducted by ICM Advisors in Italy, the brand represents on average 20 to 40 per cent of the enterprise value, with brand-driven companies peaking at 50 to 70 per cent. This finding was later confirmed by subsequent research in 2008 on Italian furniture companies in which the brand accounted for 34 per cent of the average value of the business, with peaks up to 38 per cent for the first three in the standings: Poltrona Frau, Minotti and Flexform.

Even if the brand still has difficulties in finding an accounting mechanism that expresses it in a sufficiently reliable and universally accepted way, it still represents for many companies a major asset and its estimated valuation reaches significantly high figures. Some authors estimate that the value attributed to the brand is equal to two-thirds of the company's tangible assets value.[4] The first attempt to consider the brand as a company asset started in the 1990s with Interbrand. Since then, other methodologies and specialised companies were developed. Every year, Interbrand publishes a ranking of the top-performing brands globally, called 'The Best Global Brands'. According to the 2011 Interbrand ranking, the strongest global brands are Coca-Cola, IBM, Microsoft, Google, General Electric and McDonald's, which are respectively attributed a value of 71, 69, 59, 55, 42 and 35 billion US dollars. The Interbrand methodology considers the various ways in which the brand behaves and how it adds value to an organisation based on three key aspects:

- the financial performance of the products or services offered under that brand;
- the role of the brand in the consumer buying process;
- the ability of the brand to ensure the effective achievement of expected future earnings.

Over time, this and other methodologies have been criticised for using too many subjective evaluations to determine the final value of the brand, and after comparing the scores year on year for the relative volatility of the valuations.

New methodologies were developed in order to provide a more reliable value to the brand. These try to merge objective brand equity measurements obtained with ad hoc consumer research, with financial indicators accepted by the international financial community. For some years now, for example, Millward Brown Optimor in collaboration with The Financial Times, Bloomberg and Datamonitor ranks the 100 most powerful brands (BrandZ Top 100 Most Powerful Brands, see Chapter 2). According to this approach, brands with loyal customers are likely to be characterised by higher values, and those with a high 'Brand Voltage' (an indicator based on a combination of brand loyalty and willingness to buy) have more opportunities to grow their value. According to the 2011 BrandZ Top 100 Most Valuable Global Brands classification, the strongest ones in order are Apple, Google, IBM, McDonald's, Microsoft and Coca-Cola, which are respectively attributed a value of 153, 111, 100, 81, 78 and 73 billion US dollars.

It is worth noting that although the value attributed by the two studies in some cases is quite different (e.g. according to BrandZ, Google is worth almost double what was estimated by Interbrand), seven of the top ten brands are the same in both research studies.

In conclusion, although a lot remains to be done to estimate the value of a brand in a reliable manner and correctly placing it within financial statement items, its importance within the company's intangible assets remains indisputable.

NOTES

INTRODUCTION

1. Jacobson and Mizik (2009).
2. Pioneers in the study of the processes of creation of high symbolic value brands have been the contributions of Ravasi and Rindova (2008) and Dalpiaz, Rindova and Ravasi (2010). Other contributions have analysed specific categories of high symbolic value brands that have defined *cult* and *icon* brands.

1 BRANDS AND SOCIAL IDENTITIES: AN INCREASINGLY STRONG CONNECTION

1. See Hofstede (1980), Markus and Kitayama (1991), and Brewer and Gardner (1996).
2. These are the main conclusions of the famous American sociologist Richard Sennett about new capitalism in his book, *The Corrosion of Character: The Personal Consequences of Work in the New Capitalism* (1998).
3. Rifkin (2001).
4. Rifkin (2001).
5. Berger and Heath (2007).
6. See www.tedpolhemus.com; Cova (1997), Cova and Cova (2001).
7. Fournier (1998).
8. http://www.wolffolins.com/
9. Klein (2000).
10. Porter and Kramer (2011).
11. Chernev, Hamilton and Gal (2011).

2 THE BRAND: WHAT IT IS, HOW IT BUILDS VALUE AND WHY WE GROW FOND OF IT

1. Aaker (1997).
2. Kapferer J.N., Les marques, capital de l'entreprise, Les Editions d'Organisation, 1991; Strategic Brand Management. New Approaches to Creating and Evaluating the Brand Equity, Free Press, 1994.
3. Semprini (1993).
4. Kotler and Keller (2006).
5. Aaker (1997).
6. Keller (1993).
7. Maslow (1968).
8. Aaker (1996).
9. Davis (2002).
10. Starting in 1993, more than 35,000 brands were evaluated by consulting more than 500,000 consumers in 46 countries.
11. Both the Brand Asset Valuator and BrandZ, as do other theories, try to find a correlation between the brand and its economic performance or value assets. This aspect will be further discussed by us in the Appendix.
12. Starting in 1988, more than 60,000 brands were evaluated by consulting more than 1.5 million consumer in more than 30 countries.
13. Carroll and Ahuvia (2006).
14. Batra, Ahuvia and Bagozzi (2012).
15. Oxford Dictionaries, www.oxforddictionaries.com
16. Ragas and Bueno (2002).
17. Grant and Wipperfürth (2002), http://www.mindcontrol101.com
18. Holt (2004).
19. Millward Brown – 'What makes an Iconic Brand' (2009).

3 FROM AUTHORITY TO LIFESTYLE: A MAPPING OF SYMBOL INTENSIVE BRANDS

1. Aaker (2009).
2. Holt (2004).
3. The myth is explained by Sonny Barger in the book Hell's Angel: The Life and Times of Sonny Barger and the Hell's Angels Motorcycle Club (2001).
4. Semprini (1993).
5. Aaker and Keller (1990).
6. 'L'anima di gomma di Pzero' [Pzero's rubber soul] (2011).

4 HOW LIFESTYLE BRANDS WORK: AN INTERPRETATIVE MODEL

1. For further details, see Shulman and Mosak (1988), Adler (1931) and Bourdieu (1984).
2. Bell (1958), pp. 225–42.
3. Rainwater, Coleman and Handel (1959).
4. Havighurst and Feigenbaum (1959).
5. Plummer (1974).
6. Featherstone (1991).
7. Chernev, Hamilton and Gal (2011).
8. Branson (1999), http://www.virgin.com/people-and-planet/our-vision.
9. Casetti and Di Chio (1990).
10. Heath and Heath (2007).
11. First spoken of in Jenkins (2006).
12. *Journal of Design*, 1(1), 2007, 160.
13. Schultz and Jones Yang (1997).
14. 'Nike does more than outfit the world's best athletes. We are a place to explore potential, obliterate boundaries, and push out the edges of what can be. We're looking for people who can grow, think, dream and create. We thrive in a culture that embraces diversity and rewards imagination. We seek achievers, leaders and visionaries. At Nike, it's about bringing what you have to a challenging and constantly evolving game' (source: company website).
15. 'Patagonia enjoys employing individuals who are active in the surfing, outdoor, and environmental community' (source: job posting, 2011).
16. Heskett et al. (1997) and Heskett et al. (2003).

5 THE MODEL IN ACTION

1. Information and quotes are from Johnson (2005) and Isaacson (2011).
2. Johnson (2005).
3. The quotes by Renzo Rosso are taken from his book *Be Stupid For Successful Living* (2011).
4. The Only the Brave Group controls the Diesel brand, and through the industrial company Staff International produces and distributes under licence brand such as DSquared2, Maison Martin Margiela, Marc Jacobs men, Vivienne Westwood, Viktor & Rolf and Just Cavalli.
5. Rosso (2011).

6. Rosso (2011).
7. Information and quotes are from 'Patagonia, From the ground up', *Entrepreneur*, 12 May 2010; 'Reflections of a green business pioneer', a lecture by Yvon Chouinard, UCLA, 2 May 2011; 'Patagonia & American apparel set the stage for U.S. clothing industry to go organic', *Business Times*, 5 December 2006; Lewis (2010).
8. From a Patagonia product catalogue: www.patagonia.com/us/patagonia.go?assetid=3351
9. Casey (2007).
10. Article 13, CSR Best Practice – Patagonia, November 2006: http://www.article13.com/A13_ContentList.asp?strAction=GetPublication&PNID=1245
11. Information and quotes are from Popham (2009), Hopkins (2003), Van Der Meulen (2008), Petrini and Padovani (2005).
12. Presidia (singular Persidium) are projects run by the Slow Food Foundation for Biodiversity to offer artisan food producers concrete assistance.
13. Ark of Taste is a project to rediscover, catalogue, describe and publicise food products or species that have been forgotten or are threatened worldwide. Today the forgotten foods list includes 1,000 products from more than 50 countries.
14. From the 1986 Manifesto, available at www.slowfood.com/international/2/our-philosophy
15. See Andrews (2010).
16. http://www.slowfood.it
17. http://www.slowfood.com/about_us/eng/mainfesto.lasso
18. Radio 24 Live by Sole 24 Ore, *Storielle*: interview of Carlo Petrini by Roberta Giordano, 7 June 2009.

APPENDIX

1. Davis (2002).
2. ICM Advisors, www.icmadvisors.eu
3. Gerzema, Lebar and Rivers (2009).
4. Aaker (1991).

BIBLIOGRAPHY

Aaker, D., *Brand Equity*, Milan, Franco Angeli, 1997.

Aaker, D. A., *Managing Brand Equity: Capitalizing on the Value of a Brand Name*, New York: The Free Press, 1991.

Aaker, D. A., *Building Strong Brands*, New York: The Free Press, 1996.

Aaker, D. A., 'Beyond functional benefits', *Marketing News*, 30 September 2009.

Aaker, D. A., *Brand Relevance: Making Competitors Irrelevant*, San Francisco: Wiley, 2011.

Aaker, D. A. and Joachimsthaler, E., *Brand Leadership*, New York: The Free Press, 2000.

Aaker, D. A. and Keller, K. L., 'Consumer evaluations of brand extensions', *Journal of Marketing*, 54, 1990, 27–41.

Adler, A., *What Life Could Mean to You*, Center City, MN: Hazelden, 1931.

American Marketing Association, *Marketing Definitions: A Glossary of Marketing Terms*, Chicago, IL: AMA, 1960.

Andrews, G., *Slow Food*, Bologna: IL Mulino, 2010.

Azoulay, A. and Kapferer, J. N., 'Do brand personality scales really measure brand personality?', *Journal of Brand Management*, 11(2), 2003, 143–55.

Barger, S., *Hell's Angel: The Life and Times of Sonny Barger and the Hell's Angels Motorcycle Club*, New York: HarperCollins, 2001.

Batra, R., Ahuvia, A. and Bagozzi, R. P., 'Brand love', *Journal of Marketing*, 76(2), March 2012, 1–16.

Bell, W., 'Social choice, life styles, and suburban residence', in *The Suburban Community*, William M. Dobriner (ed.), New York: G. P. Putnam's Sons, 1958, pp. 225–47.

Berger, J. and Heath, C., 'Where consumers diverge from others: Identity signaling and product domains', *Journal of Consumer Research*, 34, 2007, 121–34.

Bourdieu, P., *Distinction: A Social Critique of the Judgement of Taste*, trans. R. Nice, Cambridge, MA: Harvard University Press, 1984.

Branson, R., *Losing My Virginity: How I've Survived, Had Fun, and Made a Fortune Doing Business My Way*, New York: Three Rivers Press, 1999 (http://www.virgin.com/people-and-planet/our-vision).

Branson, R., *Screw Business as Usual*, New York: Portfolio/Penguin, 2011.

Brewer, M. B. and Gardner, W., 'Who is the "We"? Levels of collective identity and self representations', *Journal of Personality and Social Psychology*, 71(1), 1996, 83–93.

Bush, M., *Adidas Lets Consumers Help With Originals Brand Building*, Advertising Age, February 4, 2008.

Carroll, B. A. and Ahuvia, A. C., 'Some antecedents and outcomes of brand love', *Marketing Letters*, 17(2), 2006, 79–89.

Casetti, F. and Di Chio, F., *Analisi del film*, Milan: Strumenti Bompiani, 1990.

Casey, S., 'Blueprint for green business', *Fortune*, 29 May 2007.

Chernev, A. Hamilton, R. and Gal, D., 'Competing for consumer identity: Limits to self-expression and the perils of lifestyle branding', *Journal of Marketing*, 75(3), May 2011.

Chouinard, Y., *Let My People Go Surfing*, New York: The Penguin Press, 2005.

Corbellini, E. and Saviolo, S., *Managing Fashion and Luxury Companies*, Milan: Etas Milano, 2009.

Cova, B., 'Community and consumption: Towards a definition of the linking value of products or services', *European Journal of Marketing*, 31(3), 1997, 297–316.

Cova, B. and Cova, V., 'Tribal aspects of postmodern consumption research: The case of French in-line roller skates', *Journal of Consumer Behavior*, 1(1), 2001, 67–76.

Dalpiaz, E., Rindova, V. and Ravasi, D., 'Where strategy meets culture: The neglected role of cultural and symbolic resources in strategy research', in *Advances in Strategic Management: The Globalization of Strategy Research*, J. Baum and J. Lampel (eds), 27, 2010, 175–208.

Davis, S., *Brand Asset Management: Driving Profitable Growth Through Your Brands*, San Francisco: Jossey-Bass Business & Management, 2002.

Denizet-Lewis, B., *The Man Behind Abercrombie & Fitch*, Salon.com, 2006.

Desmet, P. and Hekkert, P., 'Framework of product experience', *International Journal of Design*, 1(1), January 2007, 57–66.

Featherstone, M., *Consumer Culture and Postmodernism*, London: Sage Publications, 1991.

Fournier, S., 'Consumers and their brands: Developing relationship theory in consumer research', *Journal of Consumer Research*, 24(4), 1998, 342–73.

Fournier, S. and Alvarez, C., 'Brands as relationship partners: Warmth, competence, and in-between', *Journal of Consumer Psychology*, 22(2), 2012, 177–85.

Gerzema, J., Lebar, E. and Rivers, A. 'Measuring the contributions of brand to shareholder value (and how to maintain or increase them)', *Journal of Applied Corporate Finance*, 21(4), Fall 2009, 79–88.

Grant, J. and Wipperfürth, A., *How Cults Seduce*, 2002 (www.scribd.com/doc/35582827/Cult-Branding).

Havighurst, R. J. and Feigenbaum, K. 'Leisure and life style,' *American Sociologist*, 64, 1959, 396–404.

Heath, C. and Heath, D., *Made to Stick*, New York: Random House, 2007.

Heskett, J., Sasser, W. E. and Schlesinger, L., *The Service Profit Chain: How Leading Companies Link Profit and Growth To Loyalty, Satisfaction and Value*, New York: The Free Press, 1997.

Heskett, J. L., Sasser, W. E. and Schlesinger L., *The Value Profit Chain: Treat Employees Like Customers and Customers Like Employees*, New York: The Free Press, 2003.

Hofstede, G. H., *Culture Consequences: International Differences in Work-related Values*, London: Sage Publications, 1980.

Holt, D., *How Brands Become Icons: The Principles of Cultural Branding*, Boston, MA: Harvard Business School Press, 2004.

Hopkins, J., 'Slow Food movement gathers momentum', *USA Today*, 25 November 2003.

Isaacson, W., *Steve Jobs*, New York: Simon & Schuster, 2011.

Jacobson, R. and Mizik, N., 'Valuing branded businesses', *Journal of Marketing*, 73(6), 2009, 137–53.

Jenkins, H., 'Transmedia storytelling', *MIT Technology Review*, January 2003.

Jenkins, H., *Convergence Culture: Where Old and New Media Collide*, New York: New York University Press, 2006.

Johnson, B., 'The coolest player in town', *The Guardian*, 22 September 2005.

Kapferer, J. N., *Strategic Brand Management: New Approaches to Creating and Evaluating the Brand Equity*, New York: The Free Press, 1994.

Kapferer, J. N., *The New Strategic Brand Management: Advanced Insights and Strategic Thinking*, fifth edition, London: Kogan Page, 2012.

Kapferer, J. N. and Thoenig, J. C., *Les marques: Capital de l'entreprise*, Paris: Éditions d'Organisation, 1991.

Katz, D., *Just Do It: The Nike Spirit in the Corporate World*, Holbrook, MA: Adams Media Corporation, 1994.

Keller, K. L., 'Conceptualizing, measuring, and managing customer-based brand equity', *Journal of Marketing*, 57, January 1993, 1–22.

Keller, K. L., *Strategic Brand Management: Building, Measuring, and Managing Brand Equity*, Upper Saddle River, NJ: Prentice Hall, 1998.

Keller, K. L. 'Managing brands for the long run: Brand reinforcement and revitalization strategies', *California Management Review*, 41(3), 1999, 102–24.

Keller, K. L., 'Understanding the richness of brand relationships: Research dialogue on brands as intentional agents', *Journal of Consumer Psychology*, 22(2), 2012, 186–90.

Klein, N., *No Logo: Taking Aim at the Brand Bullies*, New York: Picador, 2000.

Kotler, P. and Caslione, J., *Chaotics: The Business of Managing and Marketing in The Age of Turbulence*, New York: AMACOM, 2009.

Kotler, P. and Keller, K. L., *Marketing Management*, 12th edition, Upper Saddle River, NJ: Prentice Hall, 2006.

'L'anima di gomma di Pzero' [The soul Pzero rubber], Press Release, 21 September 2011.

Lewis, M., 'Catching up with: Patagonia's Jenn Rapp on Environmental Initiatives', *Transworld Business*, 8 April 2010.

Markus, H. and Kitayama, S., 'Culture and the self: Implications for cognition, emotion, and motivation', *Psychological Review*, 98(2), 1991, 224–53.

Maslow, A., *Toward a Psychology of Being*, second edition, New York: John Wiley & Sons Inc., 1968.

Millward Brown Optimor, *Top 100 Most Valuable Global Brands*, 2010.

Park, J. K. and Roedder, J. D., 'Got to get you into my life: Do brand personalities rub off on consumers?,' *Journal of Consumer Research*, 37(4), 2010, 655–69.

'Patagonia, From the ground up', *Entrepreneur*, 12 May 2010.

'Patagonia & American Apparel set the stage for U.S. clothing industry to go organic', *Business Times*, 5 December 2006.

Petrini, C. and Padovani, G., *Slow Food Revolution: Da Arcigola a Terra Madre. Una nuova cultura del cibo e della vita*, Milan: Rizzoli, 2005.

Plummer, J. T., 'The concept and application of lifestyle segmentation', *Journal of Marketing*, 38(1), 1974, 33–7.

Popham, P., 'Carlo Petrini: The Slow Food gourmet who started a revolution', *The Independent*, 10 December 2009.

Porter, M. and Kramer, M., 'The big idea: Creating shared value', *Harvard Business Review*, (1), January/February, 2011.

Ragas, M. W. and Bueno, B. J., *The Power of Cult Branding*, New York: Crown Business, 2002.

Rainwater, L., Coleman, R. P. and Handel, G., *Workingman's Wife*, New York: Oceana Publications, 1959.

Ravasi, D. and Rindova, V., 'A cultural perspective on value creation', in *Handbook of Emerging Approaches to Organization Studies*, D. Barry and H. Hansen (eds), London: Sage Publications, 2008.

'Reflections of a green business pioneer', a Lecture by Yvon Chouinard, UCLA, 2 May 2011.

Rifkin, J., *The Age of Access: The New Culture of Hypercapitalism, Where All of Life is a Paid-for Experience*, New York: Tarcher, 2001.

Roberts, K., *Lovemarks*, New York: PowerHouse Books, 2005.

Rosso, R., *Be Stupid for Successful Living*, Milan: Rizzoli, 2011.

Semprini, A., *Marche e mondi possibili: Un approccio semiotico al marketing della marca*, Milan: Franco Angeli, 1993.

Sennett, R., *The Corrosion of Character: The Personal Consequences of Work in the New Capitalism*, New York: Norton, 1998.

Shulman, B. H. and Mosak, H. H., *Manual for Life Style Assessment*, Muncie, IN: Accelerated Development, 1988.

Shultz, H. and Jones Yang, G., Pour your heart into it: How starbucks built a company one cup at a time, Hyperion, 1997.

Smit, B., *Sneaker Wars*, New York: HarperCollins, 2008.

Van Der Meulen, H. S., 'The emergence of Slow Food: Social entre-preneurship, local foods, and the Piedmont gastronomy cluster', in *Pathways to High-tech Valleys and Research Triangles: Innovative Entrepreneurship, Knowledge Transfer and Cluster Formation in Europe and the United States*, W. Hulsink and H. Dons (eds), New York: Springer, 2008, pp. 225–47.

Veblen, T., *The Theory of the Leisure Class*. Penguin twentieth-century classics, London: Penguin Books, 1994 [1899].

INDEX

CPSIA information can be obtained
at www.ICGtesting.com
Printed in the USA
LVOW04*0728171017

552728LV00008BA/57/P